# mend & make
# FABULOUS

First published in the United States by

Interweave
A division of F+W Media
201 East Fourth Street
Loveland, CO 80537
www.interweave.com

ISBN: 978-1-62033-534-5

Library of Congress Cataloging-in-Publication Data not
available at time of printing.

COMMISIONING EDITOR: Isheeta Mustafi
PROJECT EDITOR: Cath Senker
ASSISTANT EDITOR: Tamsin Richardson
ART DIRECTOR: Lucy Smith
ART EDITOR: Jennifer Osborne
DESIGN: Paul Kayser & Michelle Rowlandson
COVER DESIGN: Julia Boyles
TUTORIAL PHOTOGRAPHY: Madeleine Boardman,
Kin Hai & Shane Mahood
PICTURE RESEARCH: Heidi Adnum

# mend & make
# FABULOUS

### sewing
### solutions
### &
### fashionable
### fixes

## DENISE WILD

INTERWEAVE.
interweave.com

# Contents

Vintage dress with embroidered detail
and belt as featured in Chariot Marie's
Etsy shop.

# HOW TO USE THIS BOOK

Whether it's a designer splurge, a go-to basic, or a cherished vintage piece, a true fashion devotee strives to keep all of their clothes looking as good as new. And if you love your carefully edited wardrobe like I do mine, you understand that the ability to repair, revive, and even revamp a garment is priceless.

With this book, I'll show you how! Not only will you learn mending basics, including stitching holes, hemming, and replacing zippers, I'll also show you how adding some creativity to your newly found repair skills will make your clothes even more fabulous than they were the first time around. The best part? This book is for everyone! You don't need to be a sewing or DIY superstar to keep your wardrobe looking luxe.

Chapters are divided according to the garment glitches you might run into, whether it's washed-out coloring on your favorite jeans or a hole or snag in a sheer blouse. Each chapter has a series of tutorials detailing how to solve each problem—the tutorials here use contrasting thread to show the repair clearly, but generally you will need to use matching thread. I also walk you through "fabulous" options— some inspired alternatives to the standard fixes, including techniques like beading, adding lace, and creating couture-style weighted seams.

*Denise*

**Denise is the founder of LoveSewing and The Sewing Studio, and Content Director of BurdaStyle.**

## MEND IT

These are the "straight" mending pages. They show you what the problem might be and explain all the ways in which you might be able to fix it.

## *Make it Fabulous*

These are the "fabulous" pages. Aside from tutorials, they also give you a hit of inspiration and ideas for some of the great things you can do to make your clothes even better than before.

# RUNS, RIPS & FLAWS

Clockwise from left: Knit ASOS cardigan, Nasty Gal croptop, and Minkpink shorts as featured on Cindy Chi's blog; Studded ombre denim shorts designed by Natalie W for her Etsy shop; Glitzy Birdie shirt and lace badge cardigan by iAnyWear as featured on Mayo Wo's blog.

# MEND IT **TORN WOVEN FABRIC**

When you notice a tear in woven fabric, it's important to fix it right away before it gets any larger. Fortunately, torn woven fabric is easy to mend using fusible interfacing to patch the tear.

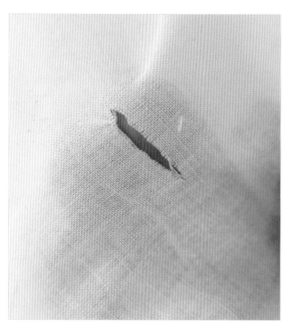

Interfacing is a textile that is used to add body and stability within certain areas of a garment, usually at collars, cuffs, waistbands, and facings. Here, you'll use interfacing like an inside patch. Fusible interfacing has a heat-activated adhesive on one side, so you just iron it in place.

### WOVEN FABRICS

Woven fabrics are made up of intersecting threads that are perpendicular to each other. They tend to be very durable, and are often used in garments because of their ability to maintain their shape after being cut. Woven fabrics can range from cotton and linen to satin and georgette, and they usually fray when torn.

## TIPS

- If your fabric is light, choose white interfacing, and if it's a dark color, use black interfacing.
- Use lightweight interfacing when repairing lightweight fabric (such as georgette) and medium-weight interfacing for medium-weight fabric (such as a linen blend).

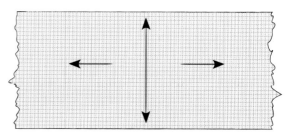

# SOLUTION: PATCH WITH INTERFACING

1. Trim any spare threads and frayed fibers from around the tear.

2. Cut a piece of fusible interfacing 1" (2.5 cm) longer and 1" (2.5 cm) wider than the tear.

3. Place the fusible interfacing, glue side up, on an ironing board, and lay the wrong side of the torn fabric over the interfacing.

4. On the right side of the fabric, match up the raw edges of the tear as best you can.

5. Press and hold an iron on the right side of the tear. (For delicate fabrics that may scorch or alter with heat, put a cotton pressing cloth between the fabric and the iron.)

6. The heat will stick the interfacing to the fabric, keeping the tear closed.

# MEND IT **TORN KNIT FABRIC**

Knit fabrics are generally tricky to work with, especially for new sewers, because they're stretchy. Here's a quick, simple, updated way to mend your torn knit fabric.

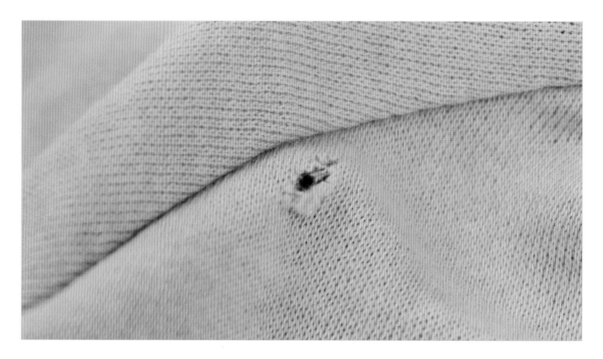

Normally, you would sew a knit fabric using a stretch stitch on a sewing machine, or you would use a serger (a specialty machine that sews, trims, and finishes seams in one step). However, that technique is not suitable when mending a small tear. Traditionally, people would darn holes or tears in knits. However, darning is a technical and time-consuming skill that even superstar sewers no longer really do very often these days.

**KNIT FABRICS**

Knit fabrics are made from threads that are looped together, rather than woven. While the degree of stretch is dependent on the fabric, knits are always stretchy. Double-knit fabrics have more structure and less stretch, while single-knit fabrics have a greater ability to stretch. Knit fabrics are often chosen for garments because of their ability to shape around the body, and you'll see them in a variety of garments from T-shirts to dresses.

## SOLUTION: HANDSEW CLOSED

1. Trim any spare threads from around the tear. Be careful not to unravel the fabric further.

2. Match up the raw edges of the tear as best you can. They do not need to overlap.

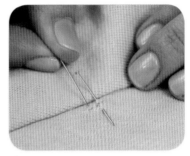

3. Pin them in place.

4. Double-thread a handsewing needle with matching thread and tie a knot at the end.

5. Handsew the tear closed from the right side of the fabric, ensuring your stitches encase the tear by at least ⅛–¼" (3–6 mm) on each side to prevent further fraying.

6. Sew your stitches on a slight slant, about ⅛" (3 mm) apart, and keep them fairly loose, which will allow your fabric room to stretch.

7. Tie your thread in a knot on the wrong side of the knit and trim the thread ends.

8. Your loose stitches allow the fabric room to stretch.

## TIP

When sewing by hand or on a machine, always use a ballpoint needle, which is designed for sewing knits. It prevents you snagging the loops of the knit fabric.

# MEND IT **TORN DENIM**

Even though we think of denim as a very durable fabric, it's often under a lot of stress through day-to-day wear and tear, and it can easily end up looking quite worn out. Once denim starts to wear out, a tear is almost always the next step. Fortunately, torn denim can be fixed in a flash by simply sewing a zigzag stitch over the tear.

Denim is a woven fabric, but it is constructed using a twill-weaving process. This means the grains of the fibers intersect on a diagonal rather than at right angles, which is the case for other woven fabrics.

You can have a right-hand or a left-hand twill, depending on the direction of the diagonal. Right-hand twill is typically smoother and flatter, whereas left-hand twill will become softer after washing it.

## SOLUTION: ZIGZAG OVER TEAR

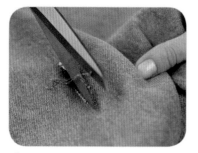

1. Trim any spare threads and frayed fibers from around the tear.

2. Match up the raw edges of the tear as best you can.

3. Pin them in place.

4. Using a zigzag stitch with a short stitch length, remove pins and sew over the tear. Use a matching thread if you don't want the repair to be visible or use contrasting thread as a design detail.

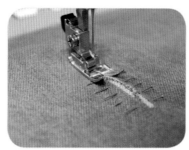

5. Adjust the stitch width as needed to make sure your zigzag stitch is encasing the tear, sewing through one side of the denim and then the other.

6. Backstitch at the beginning and end of your stitch, and trim the thread ends.

7. The finished repair makes a great design detail.

## TIP

You'll likely be using a narrow to medium stitch width for this repair. But don't get stitch width (how far your needle moves from side to side between stitches) confused with stitch length (how long each stitch is).

# MEND IT **TORN LACE**

Lace is a delicate fabric that can easily be torn during everyday wear, but those tears can be repaired in no time using simple handsewing techniques.

If the tear in your lace is small, it's best to handsew the tear closed, whereas for larger tears, the most suitable solution is to hand-appliqué a similar lace over the tear.

## SOLUTION ONE: HANDSEW CLOSED

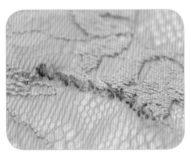

1 Starting from the wrong side of the lace where the lace pattern is tightest, bring a double-threaded needle through to the right side of the fabric and secure the knot.

2 Handstitch across the tear, following the lace pattern as best you can. If the lace is tightly woven, then stitch densely, and if it is a loose weave, stitch loosely.

3 Tie your thread in a knot on the wrong side of the lace and trim the thread ends.

## SOLUTION TWO: APPLIQUÉ LACE

1. Cut out the motif in a lace similar (in color, type, and design) to the torn lace. The appliqué should be at least ¼" (6 mm) larger than the tear all around.

2. On the right side of the fabric, place the appliqué right-side up over the tear and pin it in place, matching the designs of the two laces as best you can.

3. Double-thread a handsewing needle. Tie a knot at the end.

4. Starting from the wrong side of the main lace fabric where the lace pattern is tightest, and staying close to the edge of the appliqué, bring the needle and thread through to the right side of the fabric and secure the knot.

5. To pick stitch around the appliqué, insert the needle back down to the wrong side of the lace just a few threads over from where you started.

6. Travel ¼" (6 mm) across the wrong side of the lace before bringing the needle back up to the right side of the fabric.

7. Continue steps 5 and 6 all the way around the lace appliqué, sewing as close to the edge of the design as possible. Tie the thread in a knot on the wrong side of the lace and trim the thread ends.

8. With scissors, trim down any excess appliqué, leaving only a little bit of lace around the pick stitch you just sewed.

### TIP
Take your torn lace to the store when searching for an appliqué lace that matches, since laces have very distinctive colors, patterns, and styles.

RUNS, RIPS & FLAWS

# MEND IT **TORN SHEER FABRIC**

Sheer fabrics can be torn very easily because of their delicate qualities. Those tears can be mended using fabric glue, handsewing, or fusible interfacing.

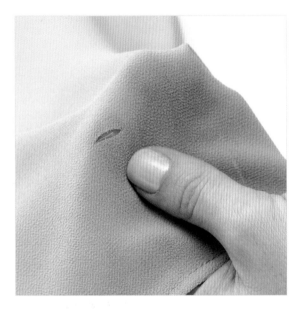

Choose a mending technique based on its finish and where the tear is located.

- Handsewing will leave a visible crease, so it's best suited for a less noticeable area such as the garment's edge.
- Fusible interfacing is best for a collar, cuff, or pocket since the extra layers of fabric will prevent the interfacing from showing through.
- Fabric glue can be used on tears in more visible locations, but first test it on an inside seam allowance to make sure it dries invisibly on the fabric.

## SOLUTION ONE: USE FABRIC GLUE

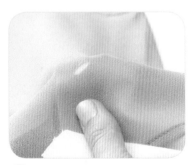

1. Place a piece of white cotton behind the tear to prevent the fabric glue from getting on another area of the garment.

2. Squeeze out a small amount of fabric glue onto the frayed edge of the tear.

3. Gently arrange the fabric so the raw edges of the tear are as close together as possible, and allow the glue to dry completely.

## SOLUTION TWO: HANDSEW CLOSED

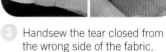

① Trim any spare threads and frayed fibers from around the tear.

② Gently pinch the right sides of the tear together and pin them in place.

③ Handsew the tear closed from the wrong side of the fabric.

## SOLUTION THREE: USE FUSIBLE INTERFACING

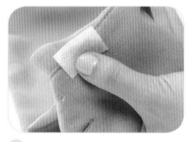

① Trim any spare threads and frayed fibers from around the tear.

② Cut a piece of fusible interfacing 1" (2.5 cm) longer and 1" (2.5 cm) wider than the tear.

③ Place the fusible interfacing glue-side up on an ironing board, and lay the wrong side of the torn fabric over the interfacing.

④ From the garment right side, match up the raw edges of the tear as best you can.

⑤ Press and hold an iron on the right side of the tear. The heat will stick the interfacing to the fabric, keeping the tear closed. Use a low heat to protect the fabric; you can also cover it with a cotton pressing cloth.

### TIP

Be careful not to touch the torn area too much—this may cause the fabric to fray or possibly tear more.

RUNS, RIPS & FLAWS

# MEND IT **SNAGGED SHEER FABRIC**

Sheer fabric is a large category that encompasses anything from chiffon and organza to tulle and georgette (shown here). Sheer simply means the fabric is so lightweight and thin that you can see through it.

The delicacy of sheer fabric is what makes it so desirable; however, it also puts it at a high risk for snags (pulls or runs). But don't let the fragility of sheers scare you off—snagged sheer fabric is easier to mend than you might think. While you should normally avoid excess handling of a fabric blemish, a snag in sheer fabric actually requires that you rub the fabric in order to repair it. Just remember to be extra gentle!

# SOLUTION: RUB IT OUT

1. Hold one finger at the start of the snag in order to provide resistance and stabilize the fabric.

2. Use another finger to rub out the snag by gently pushing the fabric across the snagged thread.

3. Continue rubbing all the way to the end of the snagged thread.

4. To eliminate any leftover bunching, press and steam the repaired snagged area using a low heat setting on your iron.

## TIPS

- Be sure to wash and completely dry your hands before rubbing out a snag since sheer fabrics absorb oils more easily than many other fabrics.
- Place a cotton pressing cloth between your garment and your iron when you're pressing delicate fabrics that could scorch or change with heat.

# MEND IT **HOLE IN SYNTHETIC FABRIC**

Holes in synthetic fabrics—including polyester, acrylic, and nylon—usually occur when the fabric melts from the heat of irons or dryers.

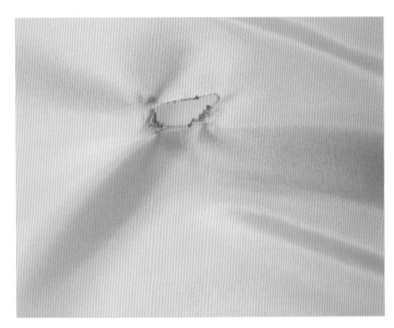

By carefully sewing an identical piece of fabric under the hole (backfilling) or over it (patching), the flaw in your synthetic fabric will become nearly invisible. Be sure to match the fabric's properties—including color and weight—in order to achieve the best result with these techniques.

## **SOLUTION ONE:** BACKFILLING

1. Trim the hole so it is symmetrical and to remove any hard areas (if it has been melted).

2. Cut the backfill fabric so it's 1" (2.5 cm) larger than the hole all the way around.

3. On the wrong side of the garment, place the backfill fabric right-side down over the hole and pin it in place.

④ From the right side of the garment, edge stitch around the hole to keep the backfill in place.

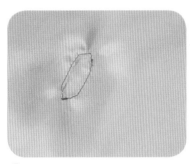

⑤ Backstitch at the beginning and end of your stitch, and trim the thread ends.

## TIPS

- Use a low heat setting or a pressing cloth when ironing.
- To reduce bulk and prevent the raw edges from fraying, singe them with a lighter.

## SOLUTION TWO: PATCHING

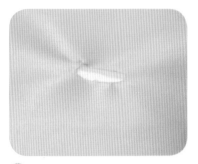

① Trim the hole to make it symmetrical and to remove any hardness (if it has been melted).

② Cut the patch fabric so it's 1" (2.5 cm) larger than the hole all the way around.

③ Turn the raw edges of the patch under ½" (1.3 cm) to the wrong side and press them with an iron. The patch is now ½" (1.3 cm) larger than the hole all the way around.

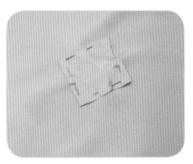

④ On the right side of the garment, place the patch right-side up over the hole and pin it in place.

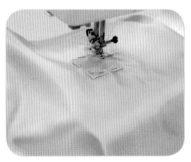

⑤ From the right side of the garment, edge stitch around the patch to keep it in place.

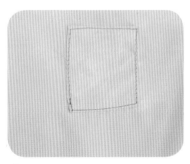

⑥ Backstitch at the beginning and end of your stitch, and trim the thread ends.

# *Make it Fabulous*

## ADD BEADING

If you're looking to add a unique design detail, or if there's a visible imperfection in your garment after it's been mended, try adding beading. Using a professional beading technique, a graphic bead design can cover a mended tear in one particular spot, or a thin row of beads can go across your garment at a snag. Choose a bead color that matches your garment for something subdued, or make a statement with a contrasting tone.

▷ See Also: Add studs, page 26

1. Determine a bead pattern based on the size and shape of the mend. Double-thread a handsewing needle and tie a knot at the end. Pick up a few fibers of the fabric with the needle and pull the needle and thread to secure the knot.

2. Add no more than two to four beads to your needle, then slide them all the way to the bottom of your thread (so they're touching the fabric).

3. As if sewing backward, enter the needle into the fabric where the beads end, and exit the needle at the initial point where you added the beads in step 2.

4. Going forward again, tunnel your needle through the opening in the beads a second time for added security, then pull your thread tight.

5. Repeat steps 2 to 4 until your design is done.

6. Tie your thread in a knot on the wrong side of your garment and trim the thread ends.

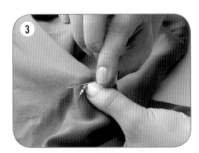

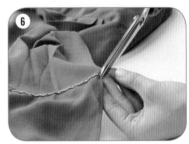

> ## Tips
>
> - Pick a bead that's a darker color than your fabric to hide a snag.
> - To prevent sheer fabric from sagging or distorting, never attach more than three or four beads at a time.

Clockwise from left: Black stretch-cotton twill jeans from Eleven's A/W with pearl detail handsewn by Ellie Rhodes; Silver-colored beads hand-stitched to denim blouse by Esther Coenen; Studs applied to sneakers by Esther Coenen; Pocket detail silk shirt with handstitching on the pockets by Lowie; Double-breasted blazer and embellished sweatshirt from J.Crew as featured on Chanel Butler's blog.

*Make it Fabulous*

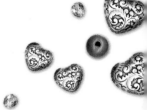

## ADD STUDS

If a rip or tear that you've mended has left a fabric blemish you now want to cover, or if you just feel like adding some edge to your garment, try adding studs. Not only can studs easily cover a fabric flaw but they also instantly add a unique style to any garment. While studs can be a great visual detail, they can be overpowering, so it is best to start with a small pattern.

▷ See Also: Go decorative, page 102

1. Draw the design for the studs directly on the right side of the fabric with a marking pencil.

2. Lay your garment flat and slide a piece of wax paper underneath, between the layers of fabric, to prevent the glue from going through it.

3. Place the iron-on studs adhesive-side down onto the markings.

4. Place a pressing cloth over the studs.

5. With your garment on an ironing board, press and hold an iron at high heat on the pressing cloth for

30 to 45 seconds. Allow the studs and fabric to cool.

6. Check that the studs have adhered. If the studs haven't stuck, repeat steps 4 and 5 until they're secured in place.

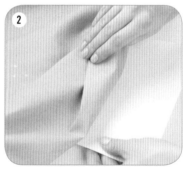

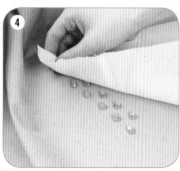

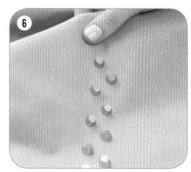

**Tip**

For long-lasting detail, make sure your studs are iron-on, rather than the type attached with glue—those are better suited to non-porous materials such as plastic, metal, and glass.

## RHINESTONES

Go glitz and try rhinestones instead of studs. Use a hot-fix applicator wand (found at your local sewing, craft, or bead store) and a tip size that corresponds with the rhinestones. Be sure to use the wand on natural fibers and blended fabrics—100% synthetic fabrics may melt from the heat.

Clockwise from left: Embellished top by Wicket featured on Mayo Wo's blog; Vintage-style tuxedo dress with vintage glass buttons designed by Maisy Brown for her Etsy site; Gem-embellished sweater by Missguided as featured on Ricarda Schernus's blog; Spike cap from Romwe as featured on Anastasia Siantar's blog.

RUNS, RIPS & FLAWS

# *Make it Fabulous*

## APPLIQUÉ LACE

Instantly turn a tear or hole into a style feature by adding a peek-a-boo lace appliqué. If you're feeling bold, cut the flaw even more for a larger lace detail! Lace can be both modern and timeless, plus it comes in a variety of colors and designs, so you can easily match or contrast any garment.

▷ See Also: Add lace, page 84

1. Cut the lace appliqué larger than the tear. Place it right-side up over the tear on the right side of the fabric. Pin it close to the edge of the lace. (If the lace has cording, pin inside the cording.)

2. Double-thread a needle with matching thread and knot the end. Starting from the wrong side of the main fabric, as close to the inside edge of the cording as possible,

bring the needle to the right side of the lace and secure the knot.

3. To pick stitch around the appliqué, insert the needle down to the wrong side of the fabric a few threads from the start.

4. Travel ¼" (6 mm) across the wrong side of the fabric and bring the needle up to the right side.

5. Repeat steps 3 and 4 all the way around the appliqué. Tie a knot on the wrong side of the fabric and trim the thread ends.

6. Trim the lace and cut away the excess fabric behind it, leaving ¼" (6 mm) around the pick stitch.

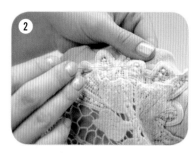

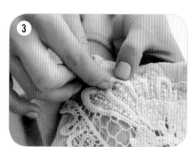

### Tip

Alençon lace has a corded edge around the detail of the lace pattern. It's the best type of lace for this technique since the cording neatly borders a single pattern and it helps hide your hand stitches.

Clockwise from left: Geometric lace insert shirt designed by Anna-Marie Cooper for her Etsy shop; Lace sweater by iAnyWear and crochet shorts by H&M featured on Mayo Wo's blog; Glitzy Birdie shirt and lace badge cardigan by iAnyWear and crochet lace shorts by Romwe featured on Mayo Wo's blog.

# *Make it Fabulous*

## PATCH IT

Why patch a fabric tear or flaw normally when you can do it in style? Add your fashion touch to any garment with a patch cut in an interesting shape or from a contrasting fabric. Play with patterns, colors, textures, and shapes, or even add a patch where it's not needed just for style's sake or as part of a larger motif.

▷ See Also: Go contrast, page 56; Be bright, page 108; Make it contrast, page 120

1. Before starting, determine the size and shape of the patch either based on the size of the tear, hole, or flaw, or based on the design you want to create.

2. Cut out the shape in a patch fabric that's similar in weight and drape to your garment.

3. On the right side of the garment, position the patch right-side up. Pin it in place close to the edges.

4. From the right side of the garment, sew the patch in place using an overedge zigzag stitch. Use a short stitch length, and adjust the stitch width based on the patch size (wide for large patches and narrow for small patches).

5. Backstitch at the beginning and end of the stitch, and trim the thread ends.

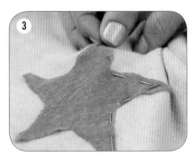

## Tips

- For a cleaner look, turn under and press the patch's raw edges to the wrong side, then edge stitch the patch in place.
- If you apply fusible interfacing to the wrong side of a patch before sewing it to the garment, it will keep its shape better.

Clockwise from left: Tribal printed denim shorts designed by Natalie W for her Etsy shop; Reindeer felted sweater designed by Miranda Anderson and featured on her blog; Heart-shaped elbow-patch sweater designed by Anna-Marie Cooper for her Etsy shop.

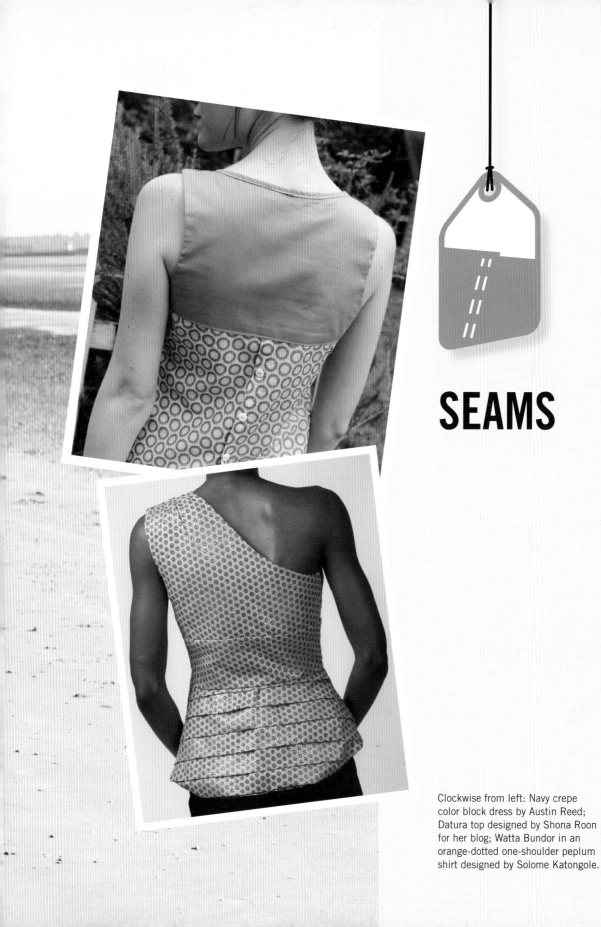

# SEAMS

Clockwise from left: Navy crepe color block dress by Austin Reed; Datura top designed by Shona Roon for her blog; Watta Bundor in an orange-dotted one-shoulder peplum shirt designed by Solome Katongole.

SEAMS

# MEND IT **HOLE IN SEAM**

A hole in a seam can show up out of nowhere. If you can access the seam from the inside, a hole can be easily sewn up with a machine.

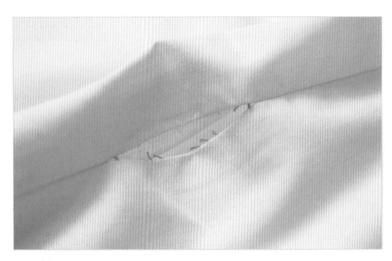

If you can't access it, use a hidden handstitch, called a ladder stitch, from the right side of the garment. When done precisely, a ladder stitch is completely invisible. For both fixes, start by removing any loose threads and frayed fibers from the unsewn area using a seam ripper or scissors.

## **SOLUTION ONE:** SEW WITH A MACHINE

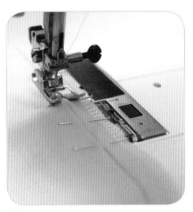

1. Place the right sides of the fabric together, matching up the seam allowances and lining up where the original seam was. Pin the fabric in place.

2. Sew the hole closed along the original seam line, overlapping any existing stitches slightly.

3. Backstitch at the beginning and end of the stitch, and trim the thread ends.

# SOLUTION TWO: LADDER STITCH

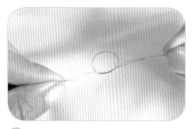

1 Double-thread a handsewing needle. Tie a knot at the end.

2 To hide your thread, knot underneath the stitch line. From the right side of your fabric, enter your needle into the seam allowance at the hole, then bring the needle through the top fold of the seam.

3 Enter the top fold of the fabric and slide the needle across the tunnel created by the fold, traveling ¼" (6 mm) with the needle before exiting the fold.

4 At the point you exited the top fold, enter the bottom fold, and travel through the bottom fold ¼" (6 mm).

5 Repeat steps 3 and 4 across the length of the hole, then pull the thread tight to close the seam.

6 Tie the thread in a knot, then push the needle in the fold of the fabric at the knot.

7 Travel 1" (2.5 cm) with the needle. Bring the needle and thread up to the right side of the fabric. Pull the needle and thread tight until the knot pulls into the seam.

8 Keeping the thread tight, trim the thread ends right at the fabric. (The thread ends will automatically pull back under the fabric and won't be visible from the right side.)

## TIP

A ladder stitch is a versatile invisible stitch that can be used to sew the opening of a cushion or even to attach a zipper. Although the stitch is hidden, you should use a thread that matches your fabric exactly.

# MEND IT **STRESSED SEAM**

Once a seam starts to stress, it will likely rip or tear fairly soon, so it's best to mend it right away. Stressed seams occur where fabric is pulled, usually in curved areas of a garment or where a lot of movement happens, including armholes, waistlines, and underseams. To properly fix a stressed seam, it is best to take out the existing seam and redo it.

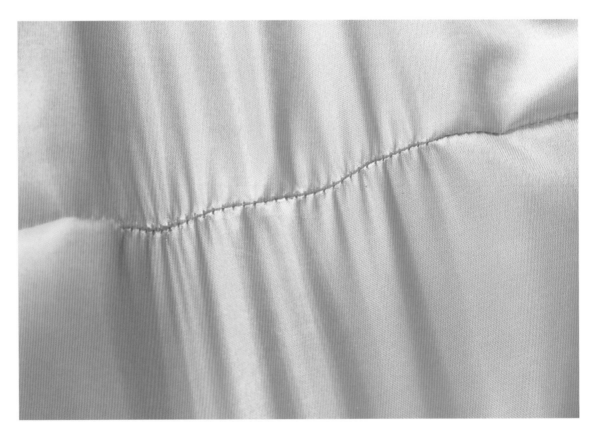

A stressed seam is a seam that is being tugged at where the fabric is pulling apart from the stitches, and the threads from the seam are visible from the right side. The key is that there's tugging, but a hole in the seam (and the fabric) has not yet developed.

## SOLUTION: REDO THE SEAM

With the right sides of the fabric together, press the stressed seam and seam allowances flat.

Draw a start and end point above and below the stressed seam with a marking pencil.

Mark a new seam line ¼" (3 mm) inside the original stressed seam (the other side of the seam allowance).

Sew along the new seam line, angling the start and end of your stitches so they taper to the start and end marks (from step 2), to overlap existing stitches. Use a short stitch length to reinforce the new seam.

Backstitch at the beginning and end of your stitch, and trim the thread ends.

Use a seam ripper or scissors to remove the original stitches from the stressed seam as well as any spare threads and frayed fibers.

Press your seam allowances open, setting the new seam.

## TIP

If your stressed seam is on a curve, once you've repaired the seam, clip into the seam allowance ¼" (6 mm) all the way around the curve to allow the fabric to move more freely.

# MEND IT **WAVY OR BUNCHED SEAM**

Waving or bunching can happen when the tension is unbalanced between the two threads that make up a seam. Side seams are especially prone to this, and the problem is most common in knit fabrics because they stretch, tugging seam stitches in different directions.

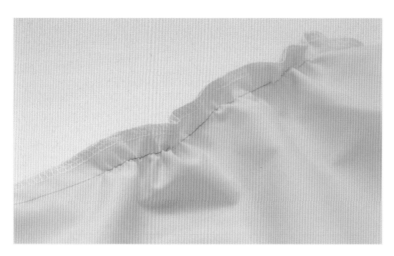

If the seam has minimal waving or bunching, you can simply pull across the thread to straighten it. However, if the waving or bunching is more substantial, you'll have to take out the troublesome seam and redo it.

## **SOLUTION ONE:** PULL ACROSS THREAD

1. Hold one finger at the start of the bunched seam in order to provide resistance and stabilize the fabric.

2. Use the finger and thumb of your other hand to gently pull the garment fabric across the thread, smoothing and straightening the bunched seam as you go.

3. To eliminate any leftover bunching, press and steam the smoothed seam area using a low heat setting on your iron.

## SOLUTION TWO: REDO THE SEAM

① Use a seam ripper or scissors to remove the stitches from the bunched area as well as any spare threads and frayed fibers.

② Place the right sides of the fabric together, matching up the seam allowances and lining up where the original seam was. Pin the fabric in place.

③ Ease in any extra fabric that may have caused the seam not to lay properly. You can easily do this by shifting the fabric between your first finger and thumb until it lays flat.

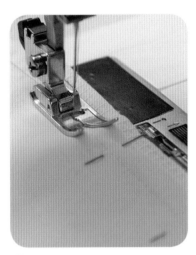

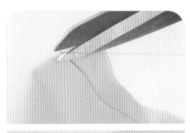

### TIP

When working with slippery fabrics, you may want to pin your fabric first then baste before sewing (basting stitch is a long running stitch). The basting will help keep the fabric layers from shifting as you sew.

④ Sew the gap closed along the original stitch line, overlapping the existing stitches.

⑤ Backstitch at the beginning and end of the stitch, and trim the thread ends.

# MEND IT **TEAR AT SLIT**

A slit in a garment is not only functional, allowing for movement, but it also adds a fun, flirty detail to your outfit. However, with stress, the stitching at the top of a slit can become weakened or even tear. When this happens, the only thing you can do is sew up the tear. You can also reinforce it to prevent the tear from happening again.

### PREVENTING A TEAR

Preventing a tear can be an easier process than fixing one. Apply fusible interfacing (see page 19) to the wrong side of the fabric at the lowest point of the seam above the slit. This will reinforce the stitching and will save you the trouble of mending a tear later on.

## SOLUTION: SEW TEAR AND REINFORCE

**1** Use a seam ripper and scissors to remove any loose threads and frayed fibers from the torn area.

**2** Place the right sides of the slit together, matching up the original seam above the slit. Pin the fabric in place.

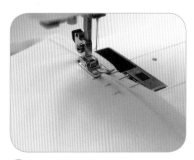

**3** Sew the tear closed along the original seam line, overlapping any existing stitches slightly.

**4** Backstitch at the beginning and end of the stitch, and trim the thread ends.

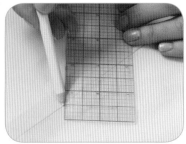

**5** Using a ruler and marking pencil, on the right side of the fabric, draw two 1½" (3.8-cm) lines at 45-degree angles from the end of the seam above the slit.

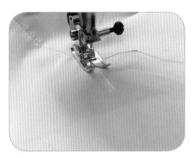

**6** Stitch directly on the 45-degree angle lines. This will hold down the slit seam allowances and reinforce the seam above the slit.

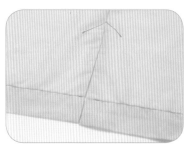

**7** Backstitch at the beginning and end of the stitches, and trim the thread ends.

### TIP
Stitching 45-degree angle lines at the end of the seam just above the slit helps prevent future tears by adding reinforcement through an intersecting seam.

# MEND IT **TWISTED SIDE SEAM**

We've all had "that shirt" where, over time, the side seam just kept twisting around to the front. Those very common twisted side seams happen because of the way the garment was cut when it was made.

Fabric naturally wants to drape straight up and down, so if it isn't prepared in the proper way before cutting, or if the pattern pieces aren't aligned accurately, the fabric will shift with multiple washings, and the side seams will twist. To fix a twisted side seam, you remove the stitches, trim the excess fabric, and even out the seam.

# SOLUTION: EVEN OUT SEAM

1. Using a seam ripper, remove the stitches from the seam you want to even out.

2. Flip the garment inside out so the fabric is right sides together, and smooth the fabric left and right so that any excess fabric at the twisted side seam sticks out.

3. Using a hip curve or a straight-edged ruler (depending on the curvature of the side seam), mark off the excess fabric by drawing along the raw edge of the smaller fabric piece with chalk.

4. Cut along the chalk line to remove the excess fabric.

5. Pin the raw edges together, keeping the fabric right sides together.

6. Sew the new side seam, overlapping any existing stitches slightly.

7. Backstitch at the beginning and end of the stitch, and trim the thread ends.

## TIP

To prevent twisted seams when sewing a garment from scratch, make sure the fabric is always pretreated and on-grain, and make sure your pattern-piece grain line is exactly parallel to the fabric's selvedge (the lengthwise grain). Use a ruler to check before pinning the pattern pieces in place.

SEAMS

# *Make it Fabulous*

## ADORN SEAMS WITH PIPING

Seams may be the last place you would think of to add extra detail. However, adorning seams with piping can add a fun, unexpected flair to an otherwise uninteresting part of a garment. Adding piping can be done with relative ease when you're already mending a seam or fixing a hole.

▷ See Also: Add piping, page 58

1. Using a seam ripper, remove the stitches from the seam you want to adorn with piping.

2. Place the right sides of the fabric together, matching up the seam allowances.

3. Sandwich the piping between the two layers of fabric, facing the piping away from the seam allowance and lining it up against the original seam.

4. Pin all of the layers in place.

5. Using a cording or piping foot on the machine, sew close to the edge of the piping through all layers. (A piping foot is extremely narrow and slides from side to side, allowing you to adjust it precisely to sew directly beside the piping.)

6. Backstitch at the beginning and end of the stitch, and trim the thread ends.

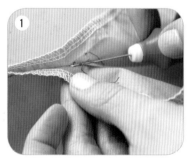

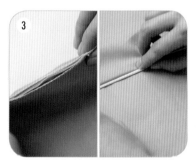

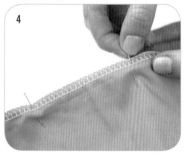

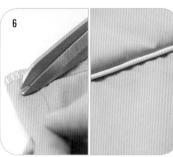

Clockwise from left: Hannah Smith in navy blue piping dress designed by Vivat Veritas; Short pencil skirt with wide band and metal zippers designed by Meisterkluft.

SEAMS

# *Make it Fabulous*

## ADD COUTURE-STYLE WEIGHTING

If you've ever experienced the hem of a garment not hanging exactly how it should, you know that it can spoil the look of your entire ensemble. Adding weight by simply attaching a small chain to the inside of the garment can help the hem hang just as it was intended to. In fact, this is how couture designers make their jackets hang well. This technique is especially helpful for garments made of tweed, wool, or bouclé.

▷ See Also: Add hardware, page 106

1. Double-thread a handsewing needle and tie a knot at the end.

2. Pick up a few fibers of the garment fabric with the needle at one edge of your hem, and bring the needle and thread through the fabric to secure the knot.

3. Loop the needle and thread through the inside hem and one link of the chain 6 to 10 times.

4. Tie your thread in a knot between the chain and the hem to keep the knot from showing inside your garment. Trim the thread ends and tie a new knot at the end of your threaded needle.

5. Repeat steps 3 and 4 every 2" (5 cm) along the entire hem of the garment. Trim off any extra chain with metal snips.

6. The completed chain, neatly sewn on the hem, can even be hidden under the lining of some garments.

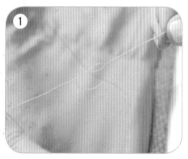

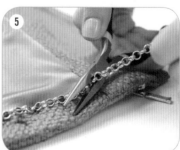
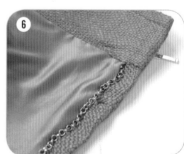

## Tip

Purchase a lightweight chain no wider than ¼" (6 mm) and ½" (1.3 cm) longer than the inside hem of the garment. You can easily find chains at a craft store or from an online retailer.

Clockwise from left: Tweed blazer from Wholesale Dress featured on Anastasia Siantar's blog; Red tweed jacket from Forever 21, gold buttons added by Chanel Butler, as featured on her blog; Blue blazer from Romwe featured on Anastasia Siantar's blog.

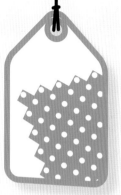

# LINING

Clockwise from left: Pauline dress
by Eucalyptus; Lingerie lace top
by Kaliko; Lace overlay skirt by
La Redoute.

LINING

# MEND IT **TORN OR FRAYED LINING**

A garment lining is constantly exposed to wear and tear, and it tends to be lighter in weight and less resilient than its corresponding outer fabric. As a result, it's very common for a lining to become torn or frayed over time.

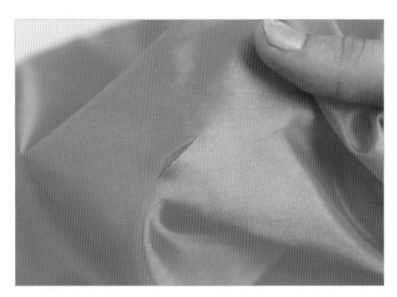

If there's a clean tear, you can mend it by either handsewing it closed or by patching it with interfacing. But if the lining is frayed at all, it's best that you handsew it closed.

## SOLUTION ONE: HANDSEW CLOSED

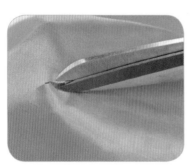

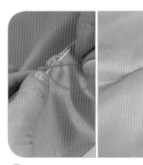

**1** Trim any spare threads and frayed fibers from around the tear.

**2** Gently pinch the right sides of the tear together and pin them in place.

**3** Handsew the tear closed from the wrong side of the lining. If you can't access the inside of the lining, sew the tear closed using a slip stitch (see page 53).

# SOLUTION TWO: PATCH WITH INTERFACING

1 Trim any spare threads and frayed fibers from around the tear.

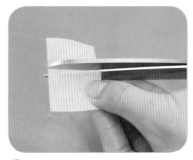

2 Cut a piece of fusible interfacing 1" (2.5 cm) longer and 1" (2.5 cm) wider than the tear.

3 Place the fusible interfacing glue-side up on a stable surface, such as an ironing board.

4 Lay the wrong side of the torn lining over the interfacing.

5 From the lining right side, match up the raw edges of the tear as best you can.

6 Cover the tear with a cotton pressing cloth to protect the lining. Press and hold an iron on the right side of the tear.

7 The heat will seal the interfacing to the lining, closing the tear.

## TIP

When you're handsewing a tear closed, be sure to use a thread that matches the fabric color so that it blends in completely. If you can't get an exact match, it is best to choose a slightly darker thread color rather than a lighter shade.

LINING

# MEND IT **LINING DETACHED FROM ZIPPER**

When you're constantly opening and closing a zipper to get in and out of your favorite piece, that extra wear can play a toll on the fabrics surrounding the zipper. In a lined garment, it's common for the lining to become detached from the zipper with extensive use. Fortunately, it can be easily fixed with a simple slip stitch.

If there's a tear in your lining AND the lining is also detached from the zipper, use a seam ripper to remove the zipper from the lining, then repair the rip in the lining with interfacing following steps 1 to 6 in Torn Woven Fabric (see page 11). Replace the zipper in the garment following steps 1–12 in Broken Zipper (see pages 100–101). Then follow the steps here to slip-stitch the lining back in place.

# SOLUTION: SLIP STITCH CLOSED

**1** Trim any spare threads and frayed fibers from around the area.

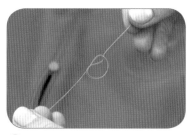

**2** Double-thread a handsewing needle. Tie a knot at the end.

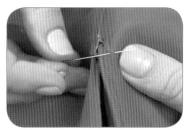

**3** From the right side of the lining, place the needle near the zipper. Bring the needle through the lining ¼" (6 mm) away. Pull the thread tight.

**4** Pick up a small amount of the zipper tape near the zipper with the needle.

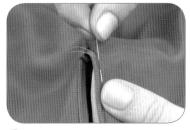

**5** Enter the fold of the lining just beside the point where you previously exited the lining, and slide the needle across the tunnel created by the fold, traveling ¼" (6 mm) before exiting the lining again.

**6** Repeat steps 4 and 5 until the lining is attached again to the zipper.

**7** Tie the thread in a knot, then push the needle in the fold of the lining at the knot. Travel 1" (2.5 cm) with the needle, then bring the needle and thread up to the right side of the lining.

**8** Pull the needle and thread tight until the knot pulls into the seam. Keeping the thread tight, trim the thread ends right at the lining. (The thread ends will automatically pull back under the lining and they won't be visible from the right side.)

## TIP

Because lining fabric is quite delicate, be sure to use a narrow needle when handsewing. That way the needle won't leave large holes that may lead to fraying.

LINING

# MEND IT **LINING DETACHED FROM HEM**

Even if you're extremely careful and follow the laundering instructions for your garments to a tee, it's still common for lining to become detached from a hem after many washes or wears.

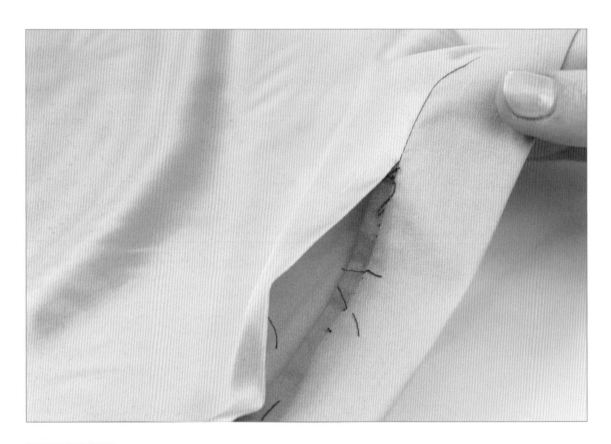

### HIDDEN STITCHES

A catch stitch is perfect for hems because it has a bit of flexibility and give. But if you'd prefer a stitch that doesn't show, try a slip stitch (see page 53), or do a blind catch stitch instead. To do this, turn back the lining and catch the underside of the lining (instead of the top) in order to hide the stitches. Using a catch stitch, a simple handsewing technique, you can easily secure your lining back in place at the hem. When a catch stitch is done properly, it will look like a series of "X"s across the inside of your garment.

# SOLUTION: CATCH STITCH CLOSED

**1** Use a seam ripper and scissors to remove any loose threads and frayed fibers from the detached area.

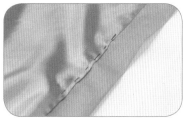

**2** Match the detached lining with the original folded lining edges and pin it in place.

**3** Double-thread a handsewing needle. Tie a knot at the end.

**4** Tunnel the needle ¼" (6 mm) through the folded edge of the hem and secure the knot.

**5** With the hem facing away from you, handsew from left to right. Enter the fabric ¼" (6 mm) over and ¼" (6 mm) above where you started (just a bit above the fold), picking up a few fibers of the fabric, and keeping your needle pointing to the left.

**6** Enter the lining ¼" (6 mm) over and ¼" (6 mm) below the step 5 point, picking up a few fibers of the fabric, and keeping your needle pointing to the left.

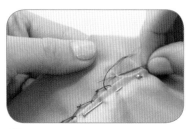

**7** Repeat steps 5 and 6, continuing to catch stitch the lining to the garment fabric along the original hemline, moving from left to right until the hem is reattached. Overlap any existing stitches slightly.

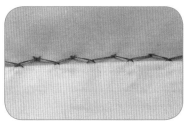

**8** Tie the thread in a knot on the wrong side of the garment and trim the thread ends.

## TIP

A catch stitch should be sewn from left to right. However, if you're left-handed, you'll find it more comfortable to sew the catch stitch from right to left.

LINING

# *Make it Fabulous*

## GO CONTRAST

An easy way to refresh a garment is to give it a new lease of life with a cool, contrast lining. To replace your existing lining with one that's high style, take out the old, copy it, and put in the new. A contrast or colorful lining (or even a notice-me print) will take any garment from standard to stand-out.

▷ See Also: Be bright, page 108; Make it contrast, page 120

1. Use a seam ripper to remove the garment's entire lining. Take note of the seam allowance measurement.

2. Separate the individual lining pieces by removing all of the seams. Take note of the seam allowance measurement, then iron each of the pieces.

3. Lay the old lining pieces on the new lining fabric, matching up the grain lines as best you can.

4. Pin the pieces in place and cut out the new lining.

5. Place the right sides of the new lining pieces together and pin them in place. Sew the new lining pieces together (backstitching at both ends), using the seam allowance measurement from step 2.

6. Place the right side of the new lining to the right side of the garment fabric and pin them together. Sew the lining to the garment using the seam allowance measurement from step 1.

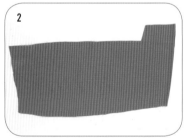

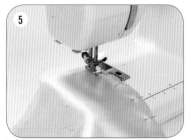

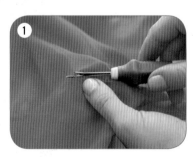

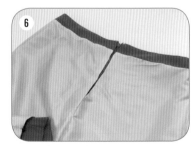

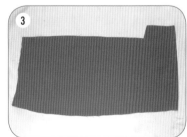

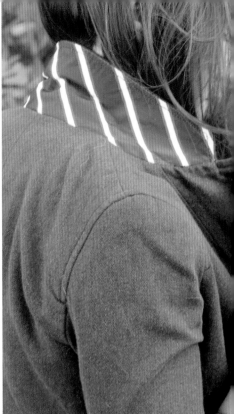

## Tip

Choose a new lining similar in weight and fabrication to the original lining in order to maintain the proper drape of your garment.

Clockwise from left: Bright, contrasting lining added by Jenna Richardson to H&M jacket; Contrast piping and lining added by Jenna Richardson to American Eagle blazer; Petticoat lining added to polka dot skirt worn by Rebecca Hawkins.

# *Make it Fabulous*

## ADD PIPING

Adding piping around your lining is a sure way to add personality to a garment. Choose a piping that matches the lining for a subtle detail or opt for a contrasting color. To add another decorative element, sew in the piping using blanket stitch.

▷ See Also: Add lace, page 84; Add ruffles, page 86

1. Remove seam stitches with a seam ripper. Put the piping between the two layers of fabric at the opening.

2. Turn the raw edge of the piping and the fabric seam allowances to one side. From the fabric right side, pin all the layers in place.

3. Double-thread a handsewing needle, and knot at the end. From under the fabric below the piping, bring the needle up to the right side, hiding and securing the knot.

4. Loop the needle and thread over the piping and stitch down through the fabric ¼" (6 mm) over and ¼" (6 mm) above where you started, but don't pull the thread tight.

5. From the fabric wrong side, bring the needle back up above the original thread directly below the point in step 3. Pull the thread tight.

6. Travel from left to right repeating steps 3 and 4, picking up a few fibers on the fold each time until the last stitch.

7. From the fabric wrong side, tie the thread in a knot and trim the ends.

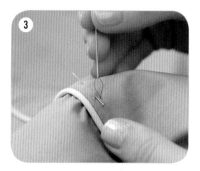
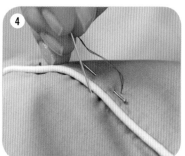

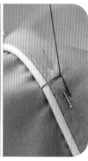
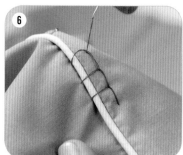
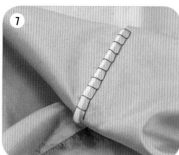

Clockwise from left: Stripes and color tote bag designed by Mandy Pellegrim; Bustier by Pull & Bear and scalloped tulip skirt by Rose Tatu featured on Mayo Wo's blog; Light, high-necked, military-style jacket designed by Meisterkluft.

# HEMS & FITTING

Clockwise from left: Printed dress by La Redoute; Dusty pink wool dress by Valentino featured on Mayo Wo's blog; White and navy gingham skirt with lace trim as featured in Chariot Marie's Etsy shop.

HEMS & FITTING

# MEND IT **STRETCHED NECKLINE**

Knit garments are notoriously prone to losing their shape, and this is especially true around the neckline. Frequent tugging and pulling can cause a neckline to stretch and distort over time.

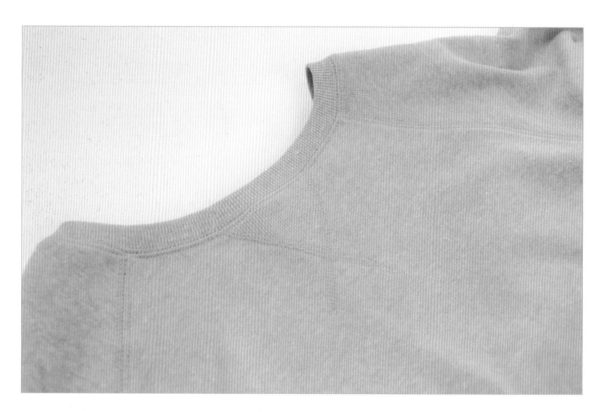

The best way to fix a neckline that has been stretched is to remove it and replace it with a brand new neckline. You can do this by sewing on ribbing, an elasticized ribbed fabric specifically made for collars, cuffs, and waistbands.

### STRETCH STITCH
A stretch stitch on the sewing machine sews like the bunny hop: the stitches go forward then backward before moving forward even more. This allows the fabric to stretch without ripping the threads. If you don't have a proper stretch stitch on your machine, use a narrow zigzag as an alternative; this will allow the fabric to stretch just slightly.

## SOLUTION: ADD NEW RIBBING

1 Using a seam ripper, remove the stretched neckline ribbing.

2 Measure the neckline of the garment (being careful not to stretch it), and cut a new ribbing to that measurement plus 1¼" (3.2 cm).

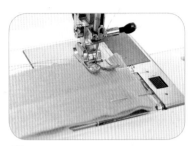

3 Using a stretch stitch on the machine, sew the ribbing's short raw edges together (right sides together) at a ⅝" (1.5 cm) seam allowance, backstitching at both ends. Trim down the seam allowance to ½" (1.3 cm). You now have a big loop.

4 With right sides together, line up the neckline raw edge with one long raw edge of the ribbing loop. Pin them together, being careful not to stretch the ribbing or the neckline.

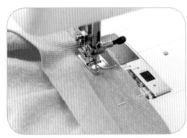

5 Using a stretch stitch on the machine, sew the ribbing in place at a ⅝" (1.5 cm) seam allowance, backstitching at both ends and trimming the threads.

6 Press the ribbing and seam allowance away from the garment. Wrap the ribbing around the seam allowance by folding it in half toward the garment wrong side.

7 Pin the new ribbing in place, making sure the raw edge of the ribbing falls below the neckline seam.

8 Topstitch on the ribbing.

### TIP

Look for new ribbing that's similar to your original neckline in weight, color, and stretch.

# MEND IT **LOOSE BODICE**

Sometimes a shirt or blouse fits overall, but the bodice is a bit too big. When you have a loose bodice that needs to be taken in a touch or needs more shape and definition, a simple solution is to add darts.

### DARTS

Darts are a way of sewing fabric together to eliminate excess fabric and add contouring around your body's curves. They'll give the bodice a more tailored and form-fitting look.

## **SOLUTION:** ADD DARTS

1 Turn the garment inside out and put it on a dress form.

2 Pinch the fabric right sides together where you would like to take the garment in. You'll want two darts (usually vertical) at even distances from the center of your body. You may want darts in the front of the bodice and also in the bodice back.

3 Where you want to take in the bodice the most, pinch the fabric right sides together. This is the fullest part of your dart. Place a pin in the bodice fabric at that point, which will become your seam line.

④ Continue placing pins along the desired seam line, tapering it at the top and the bottom.

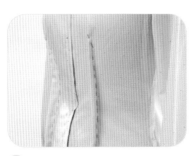

⑤ Once you've pinned the dart in place, pin the dart on the other side before taking the garment off the dress form.

⑥ Starting at the fullest part of the dart, backstitch at the beginning of the stitch and sew the dart along the pinned line.

⑦ When you get to the end of the dart, sew directly off the fabric without backstitching and leave your thread ends long.

⑧ Tie the threads in a knot and trim the thread ends, leaving a small thread tail. Repeat steps 6 and 7 down the other side of the same dart.

⑨ Press the dart flat, then to one side over a tailor's ham.

⑩ Normally, vertical darts are pressed toward the center of a garment and horizontal darts are pressed downward. Repeat steps 6 to 9 on the other dart.

## TIPS

- Enlist the help of a friend if you don't own a dress form, or pin very cautiously if you decide to do this on yourself.
- If you don't own a tailor's ham (an ironing accessory that helps prevent creases when ironing curved shapes such as the contouring created by a dart), put the dart over the curved edge of the ironing board when pressing.

# MEND IT **LONG SLEEVES**

People come in all different shapes and sizes. Unfortunately, sleeve lengths are standard for a particular shirt size and aren't customized to one's body. Instead of rolling up your long sleeves, tailor them by shortening them at the shoulder or at the cuff.

## SOLUTION ONE: SHORTEN AT THE CUFF

To shorten a long sleeve at the cuff, remove the cuff and sleeve placket (also called a gauntlet), which is the vertical detail at the sleeve vent. Note the seam allowance and any pleating. Cut off excess fabric at the sleeve end. Redo the sleeve pleats (if necessary) and create a new sleeve vent before reattaching the placket and cuff. If you're shortening ½" (1.3 cm) or less, remove and re-set the cuff without touching the sleeve placket.

## SOLUTION TWO: SHORTEN AT THE SHOULDER

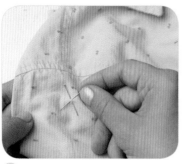

1. Determine how much of the sleeve you want to remove. Transfer that measurement from the shoulder seam going down the sleeve using pins. The center of the pin "X" marks the new sleeve cap.

2. Hand-baste along the old seam around the entire armhole, following the original curve, and going through the "X."

3. With the seam ripper, remove the sleeve from the bodice, making a note of the original seam allowance.

④ Use a French curve and marking pencil to join the hand-baste around the sleeve.

⑤ Use a sewing gauge and a different marking pencil to add the seam allowance from step 3. Cut along that new line.

⑥ Remove the threads from step 2, then sew a double baste around the sleeve cap. (To baste, sew your longest stitch, don't backstitch, and leave the threads long.)

⑦ With right sides together, pin the sleeve into the armhole, matching the underarm seams. Also match the mark from step 1 with the shoulder seam. Then pin around the bottom half of the armhole.

⑧ Gather the basting from step 6 until the sleeve cap fits into the remainder of the armhole. (To gather, see step 5 on page 86.) Pin everything in place.

⑨ Sew the sleeve to the armhole using the seam allowance from step 3. Re-finish the raw edges if needed. Repeat all steps for the other sleeve.

## TIP

To reduce gathering at the sleeve cap, make the sleeve narrower. Between steps 3 and 4, undo the top 6" (15 cm) of the sleeve seam, trim the sleeve, tapering the cut to the original seam, then re-sew it.

# MEND IT **TIGHT OR LOOSE WAISTLINE**

Waistlines can be tricky. Ideally, they would always fit perfectly, not requiring a belt or holding in your breath.

Even when a garment fits like a glove, sometimes the waistline doesn't. Adjusting a waistline requires detailed work, but it's not impossible—you can let it out or take it in to get that perfect fit once again.

## SOLUTION ONE: LET IT OUT

1. Measure the waistline of the garment and measure your waist where you want the waistline to sit.
2. Calculate the difference between the measurements in step 1, and divide that figure by four.
3. Complete steps 1 and 2 from "Take it in" (see page 69).

4. With the garment inside out, start from the side seam and mark the measurement from step 2 in the seam allowance on both sides. Draw new seam lines at that measurement, tapering the bottom of the lines so they meet the existing side seams.
5. Complete step 6 from "Take it in."
6. Use a seam ripper to remove original seams (only where a new seam has been sewn).
7. Press the seams open, then complete steps 8 and 9 from "Take it in."

# SOLUTION TWO: TAKE IT IN

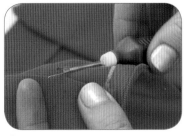

1 Use a seam ripper to remove stitches that are holding the facing of the waistband in place at the sides. (Facing is the strip of right-side fabric that touches your skin.)

2 Open the facing and flip it away from the garment.

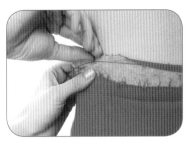

3 Put on the garment (or put it on a dress form) inside out, and pinch the waistline right sides together where you want to take it in, including the flipped-up facing. Put a pin in the fabric vertically.

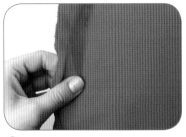

4 Place pins through the waistband facing, waistband, and on both sides of the garment along the new seam line.

5 Take the garment off, and use a marking pencil and ruler (or French curve) to mark the seam lines you pinned. Taper the bottom of the lines so they meet the existing side seams.

6 Keeping the facing opened up, sew the new side seams along the chalk line, backstitching at both ends and trimming the threads.

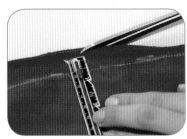

7 Cut the seam allowances to ⅝" (1.5 cm) from the new side seams, and press them open.

8 Refold the waistband and waistband facing in place and pin.

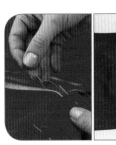

9 Handsew along the waistline to reattach the facing.

# MEND IT **STRETCHING WAISTLINE**

You know that pair of pants; when you put them on in the morning, they fit perfectly. But by the end of the day, you're constantly pulling them up.

When a waistline stretches throughout the day, it's because the fabric is losing its shape with stress and strain. This is an easy fix with twill tape, which will stabilize the waistline and prevent it from changing.

**TWILL TAPE**

Twill tape is a flat, twill-woven (usually cotton) ribbon that's available in different widths and colors and is sold either by length on a bolt or in a pre-cut package Twill tape doesn't stretch, so it helps provide stability wherever it's sewn.

## SOLUTION: ADD TWILL TAPE

**1** Start with pants that are freshly washed and dried so the waistline is exactly how you want it to fit. Measure the inside waistline of the garment and add 1" (2.5 cm).

**2** Carefully cut a piece of twill tape to this measurement.

**3** Position the twill tape inside your waistband over an existing line of stitching.

**4** Pin the twill tape to the inside of the waistband all the way around, covering the stitching.

**5** Tuck under the raw edges of the twill tape ½" (1.3 cm) on both ends.

**6** From the right side of the fabric, stitch the twill tape to the waistline by sewing directly over the existing stitch (that you covered with twill tape from the underside).

**7** Backstitch at both ends of the stitch and trim the thread ends.

**8** The twill tape will be held in place on the inside, and the extra line of stitching won't be visible on the outside since you sewed over the top of an existing line of stitches.

**TIP**
The best width twill tape for this technique is ¾" (2 cm) because it's manageable and easy to work with.

HEMS & FITTING

# MEND IT **FALLEN HEM**

A fallen hem (one that has started to come apart) can make your garment look unprofessional, sloppy, and definitely not stylish.

If your hem starts to fall, it's important to fix it right away. Thankfully, you don't need a sewing machine to fix a fallen hem—a simple needle and thread will do. There are many different hand stitches that can be used to mend a fallen hem; the three most popular are a slip stitch, catch stitch, and blind catch stitch. All can be used on a range of fabrics and are suitable for a multitude of garment fixes.

## **SOLUTION ONE:** SLIP STITCH

**1** Use a seam ripper and scissors to remove any loose threads and frayed fibers from the area of the hem that has detached.

**2** Matching up the original folded hem, pin the fallen portion in place.

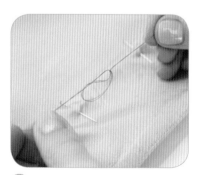

**3** Double-thread a handsewing needle. Tie a knot at the end.

④ To secure the thread knot, bring the needle through the fabric and pull the thread tight.

⑤ Push the needle into the fold of the hem, and slide the needle across the tunnel created by the fold, traveling ¼" (6 mm) before exiting the fold.

⑥ Pick up a few fibers of fabric with the needle directly above where you exited the fold.

⑦ Enter the fold again just left of where you previously exited the fold.

⑧ Repeat steps 5 to 7 until the fallen hem is mended.

⑨ Tie the thread in a knot, then push the needle in the fold of the fabric at the knot.

⑩ Travel 1" (2.5 cm) through the fold with the needle before exiting the fold.

⑪ Pull the needle and thread tight until the knot pulls into the hem. Keeping the thread tight, trim the thread ends right at the fabric. (The thread ends will automatically pull back under the fabric and they won't be visible from the right side.)

**TIP**

Take a look at the original hem to determine the hand stitch you want to use on your fallen hem.

# SOLUTION TWO: CATCH STITCH

① Use a seam ripper and scissors to remove any loose threads and frayed fibers from the detached area. Line up the original folded hem and pin the fallen portion in place.

② Double-thread a handsewing needle and tie a knot at the end. Secure the knot in the garment by passing the needle through a few threads of the fabric.

③ Working from left to right, start by tunneling the needle ¼" (6 mm) through the folded edge of the hem.

④ Enter the fabric ¼" (6 mm) over and ¼" (6 mm) above where you exited the fold, picking up a few fibers of the garment fabric, and keeping your needle pointing to the left. Pull the thread tight.

⑤ Enter the fold next, ¼" (6 mm) over and ¼" (6 mm) below step 4, keeping your needle pointing to the left and traveling through the fold ⅛" (3 mm).

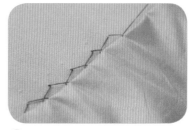

⑥ Repeat steps 4 and 5, continuing to catch stitch along the original hemline, moving from left to right, until the hem is reattached. Overlap any existing stitches slightly.

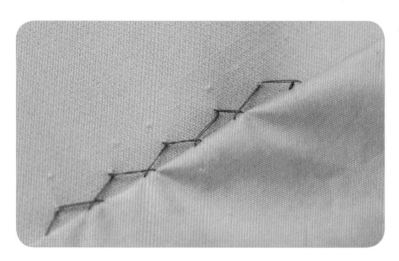

⑦ Hide your knot and thread ends in the fold of the hem by following steps 9 to 11 from Solution One (see page 72).

## SOLUTION THREE: BLIND CATCH STITCH

Follow the steps for catch stitch (Solution Two, opposite), but instead of using the top folded edge of the hem to anchor the stitches, fold back the hem about ½" (1.3 cm) and anchor the stitches inside the hem to keep them hidden. Use the pictures here as a guide.

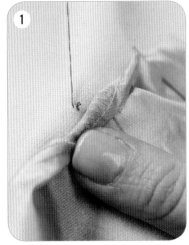

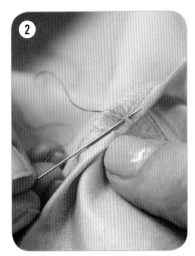

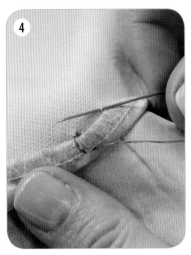

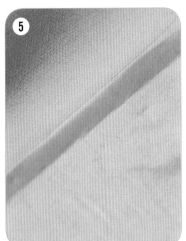

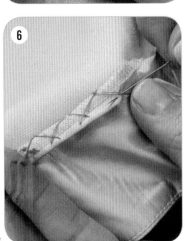

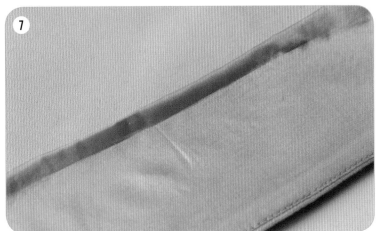

# MEND IT **LONG HEM**

When a garment's hem is too long, it can throw off the look of your entire outfit. The proper hem length can make all the difference in how a garment both looks and feels.

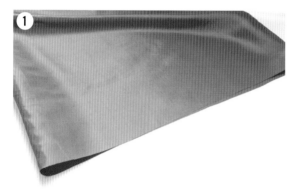

However, not all hems are created equal. Depending on the fabric and the desired finished look, you have several options for shortening a long hem:

- A topstitch hem is a simple, standard hem that can be done quickly on different garments (1).
- An original hem (often called a Euro hem) is suitable for jeans when you want to keep the store-bought distressed hem (2).
- A full hem (such as one on a circle skirt) needs to be sewn in a way that will prevent creases or puckers since you have to fit a larger circumference into a smaller one (3).

**MEASURING YOUR DESIRED HEM LENGTH**

Because we have curves, if you cut the same amount of fabric off the bottom of a skirt all the way around, the finished hem may not be even. To properly measure a finished hem length, put the garment on a dress form (or put it on and have someone assist you). Determine where you want the end of the garment to be and place a pin through the fabric horizontally at that length. This is the finished hem length. Using a yardstick placed on the floor, measure from the floor up to that pin marker. Continue transferring that measurement, measuring from the floor up, pinning at the same measurement all the way around your garment.

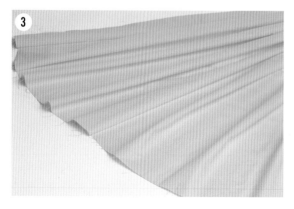

# SOLUTION ONE: TOPSTITCH HEM

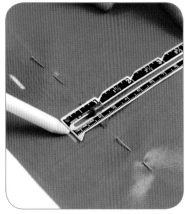

**1** From the desired finished hem length (see opposite for how to measure that), use a sewing gauge and a marking pencil to mark a ⅝" (1.5 cm) seam allowance around the hem.

**2** Cut along the marked line.

**3** Press the ⅝" (1.5 cm) seam allowance toward the wrong side of the garment. (You'll press on the finished hem marking with the seam allowance folded toward the garment inside).

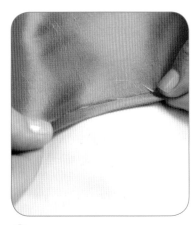

**4** Tuck the raw edge into the fold, and press again.

**5** From the inside of the garment, edge stitch around the new hem.

**6** Backstitch at both ends and trim the thread ends.

## TIP
For delicate or formal fabrics, try a slip stitch (see page 72) instead of a machine stitch.

# SOLUTION TWO: ORIGINAL HEM

**1** Determine how much shorter you want your jeans to be.

**2** Flip your jeans inside out. Starting from the top fold of the original hem, mark the measurement from step 1 around the pant leg.

**3** Fold the pant leg right sides together so the newly marked line matches up with the top fold of the original hem. Pin the fabric together.

**4** Flip your jeans right side out and remove the extension table on your sewing machine. Your pant leg will now easily slide onto the free arm.

**5** Sew all the way around the pant leg just to the right of the top fold of the original hem. Trim off the excess fabric, leaving a ⅝" (1.5-cm) seam allowance. Finish that seam allowance with an overedge zigzag. Repeat all steps for the other leg.

## TIP

When doing the original hem, you can leave the excess fabric on the inside of your pant leg (and press it in place or catch stitch to the inside of the pant leg) if you're not ready to commit to cutting it off, or if the amount you want to take off is small.

# SOLUTION THREE: EASE A FULL HEM

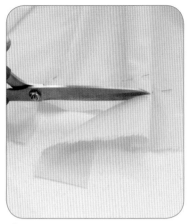

**1** From the desired finished hem length (see page 76 for how to measure it), use a sewing gauge and a marking pencil to mark a 1¼" (3.2-cm) seam allowance all the way around the hem. Remove the excess length by cutting along that marked line.

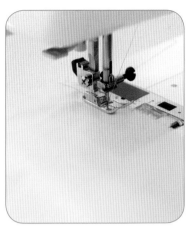

**2** Sew a baste stitch (a long machine stitch with no backstitching on either end and the thread ends left long) around the entire hem ¼" (6 mm) from the raw edge.

**3** Press the 1¼" (3.2-cm) seam allowance toward the wrong side of the garment. (You'll be pressing on the finished hem marking with the seam allowance folded toward the inside of the garment).

**4** Press again, but this time along the baste stitch, folding ¼" (6 mm) of the raw edge toward the inside of the garment.

**5** Gather the fabric along the baste stitch in order to ease the widest part of the full hem (the raw edge) into the narrower skirt portion. (See step 5 on page 86 for how to gather.) Pin the eased hem in place.

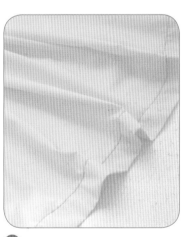

**6** From the wrong side of the garment, edge stitch along the top fold of the hem all the way around the garment, backstitching at both ends and trimming the thread ends.

# *Make it Fabulous*

## CHANGE THE SHAPE

The neckline of a top can play a big factor in your garment's style. By changing the shape of the neckline and adding a decorative element, you can easily give your top a brand-new look. Need ideas? Try binding, lace, or beaded appliqués.

▷ See Also: Appliqué lace, page 28; Patch it, page 30

1. Using a ruler or French curve, mark the shape of the new neckline with a marking pencil. Cut along the marked line, removing the excess fabric.

2. Pin your decorative element in place over the new neckline.

3. Double-thread a handsewing needle and tie a knot at the end. Starting from the wrong side of the main fabric, as close to the inside edge of the decorative element as possible, bring the needle through to the right side of the garment to secure the knot.

4. To pick stitch around the decorative element, insert the needle into the wrong side of the fabric a few threads from where you started.

5. Travel ¼" (6 mm) across the wrong side of the fabric before bringing the needle back up to the right side.

6. Repeat steps 4 and 5 all the way around the neckline, sewing as close as possible to the inside edge of the detail. Tie the thread in a knot on the wrong side of the fabric and trim the thread ends.

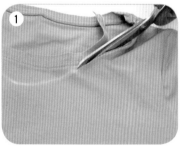

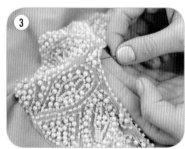

## Tip

Choose a decorative element that has a similar weight to your garment.

Clockwise from left: Sequinned cardigan by Dig, lace top by Stephie's Shop, and lemon skirt by Romwe featured on Mayo Wo's blog; Vintage black long-sleeved blouse with white polka dots as featured in Chariot Marie's Etsy shop; Lace insert button-front top designed by Anna-Marie Cooper for her Etsy shop.

# *Make it Fabulous*

## ADD A ZIPPER

Adding a zipper to your hem can be both functional and fashionable. A zipper detail can give you a little more breathing room at the bottom of the garment, or it can simply add aesthetic appeal. Add a zipper to more than one seam if you want added edge, and make sure you choose a zipper with metal teeth—the metal stands out more than plastic does.

▷ See Also: Change the closure, page 104; Change it out, page 122

1. Measure the length of the zipper from the top stopper to the bottom stopper. Usually a 5 to 8" (12.5 to 20.5 cm) zipper will look best.

2. Cut up the garment seam that same measured length. At the top of the cut, clip ⅛" (3 mm) at a 45-degree angle on both sides of the seam.

3. Press the raw edge of the cut area to the wrong side of the garment ¼" (6 mm) all the way around.

4. From the right side of the garment, place the zipper teeth-side up (and with the pull at the garment hem) underneath the cut and pressed seam area. Line up the pressed edges of fabric beside the zipper teeth, leaving a bit of the zipper tape showing.

5. Pin the zipper in place, folding back the zipper tape ends so they're tucked underneath the garment.

6. Sew the zipper in place by edgestitching around the cut and pressed area of the seam.

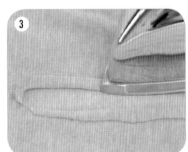
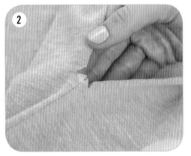
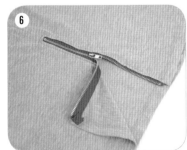
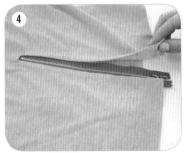
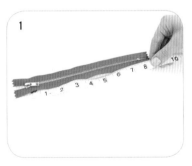
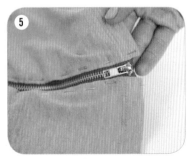

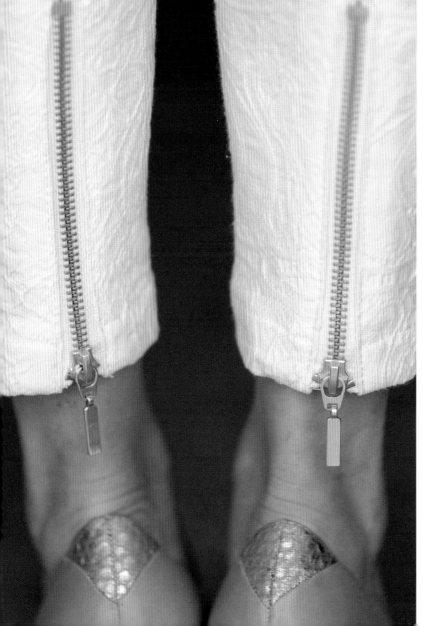

Clockwise from left: Zip detail pants by H&M featured on Kayley Heeringa's blog; Vintage detail zip jeans featured on Ricarda Schernus's blog; Brown shorts by Forever21 featured on Veronica Popoiacu's blog; Backless silk sundress with exposed zipper as featured on The Quiet House's Etsy shop.

# *Make it Fabulous*

## ADD LACE

Sewing a lace trim along a hem not only adds a feminine touch but it can also be used to hide uneven stitches or an uneven hem. With a little lace and some creative ingenuity, you can enhance a garment in a way that's both sophisticated and chic. Stay subtle with lace that's tone-on-tone, or choose a contrasting shade if you want to brighten up the hem with a pop of color.

▷ See Also: Appliqué lace, page 28

1. Measure the circumference of the hem and add 1" (2.5 cm). Cut the lace to that measurement.

2. Line up the lace so the bottom edge comes slightly below the finished hem of the garment. Pin in place.

3. Tuck under the raw edges of the lace ½" (1.3 cm) on both ends, overlapping them slightly. Pin them in place.

4. Sew the lace to the hem ¼" (6 mm) from the edge of the garment, backstitching at both ends.

5. Pin around the garment at the top of the lace, making sure the lace is lying flat against the fabric.

6. Sew the lace to the garment ¼" (6 mm) from the top edge of the lace, backstitching at both ends.

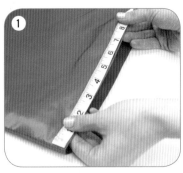

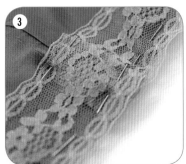

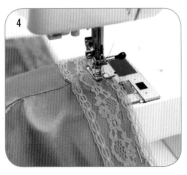

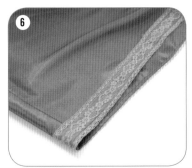

**Tip**

Use a fine needle (size 9) when sewing lace, and pretreat the lace trim before sewing it to the hem—wash and dry it just as you plan to wash and dry the finished garment.

Clockwise from left: Tie-dye tee by Romwe, crochet hem purple skirt by iAnyWear, and purse by Papermint featured on Mayo Wo's blog; Vintage white long-sleeved blouse with lace trim and pearl buttons featured in Chariot Marie's Etsy shop; White and navy gingham skirt with lace trim as featured in Chariot Marie's Etsy shop.

# *Make it Fabulous*

## ADD RUFFLES

Ruffles are a fun, flirty way to add an unexpected element of style. Choose fabric to match or contrast your garment, and sew a feminine ruffle trim to your hemline.

▷ See Also: Add lace, page 84

1. Multiply the circumference of the hem by three, and add 1¼" (3.2 cm). Decide the width of the ruffle, add ⅝" (1.5 cm), then double the total.

2. Cut fabric for the ruffle using the measurements from step 1.

3. Sew the short edges together (right sides facing) at a ⅝" (1.5 cm) seam allowance, backstitching at both ends.

4. Pin the rectangle in half (wrong sides facing) with the long edges lined up. Baste around the entire raw edge of the loop. (Sew with a long stitch, don't backstitch, and leave the thread ends long.)

5. Gather the loop fabric by holding one bobbin-thread end of the basting and gently pushing the fabric across the stitching. Do this from both ends of the baste stitch until the loop is smaller than the hem.

6. Pin the loop and hem right sides facing, lining up the raw edges and evenly distributing the gathers. Sew using a ⅝" (1.5 cm) seam allowance, backstitching at both ends.

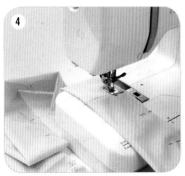
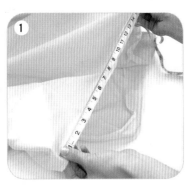
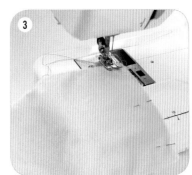

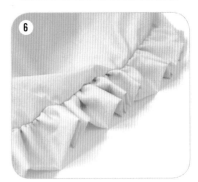

## Tip

To distribute the gathers
evenly, pin the center front
and the center back of the
hem and the ruffle together.
Find the center of those two
sections and pin. Repeat this
again. Ease out the ruffles
until the gathers are spread
out evenly. Pin in place.

Clockwise from left: Black short skirt
by La Redoute; Vintage blue ruffle
dress with brown belt featured on
Chariot Marie's Etsy shop; Vintage
bright yellow dress as featured on
Claude Monique Viard's blog; Ruffled
Franconi skirt made with vintage fabric
designed by East of Grey.

# CLOSURES

Clockwise from left: Spotty peplum blouse with floral collar by Lowie; Floral bandage skirt by Soeurs featured on Anastasia Siantar's blog; Crepe overall by Eliana for her Etsy shop.

CLOSURES

# MEND IT **MISSING BUTTON**

Whether it is due to wear and tear or simply getting caught and pulled off, buttons often disappear without a trace.

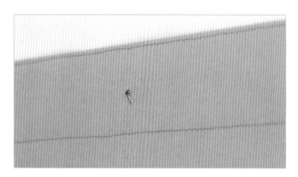

Replacing a missing button can be easily done, but the secret is to use more than just a needle and thread. There are a few key tricks (and some tools at home) that will help you sew a button that won't budge.

## **SOLUTION:** REPLACE BUTTON

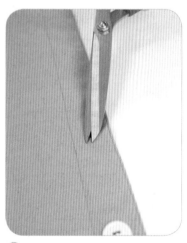

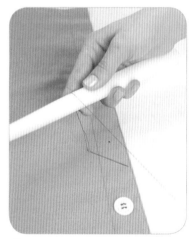

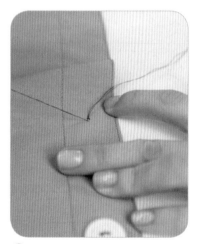

1. Use scissors to snip away the original threads.

2. Double-thread a handsewing needle and tie a knot at the end. Then pull the thread across a taper candle to coat it in wax. This helps strengthen the thread to keep the button in place.

3. From the right side of the garment, pass the needle through a few threads of the top fabric only and secure the knot. This will hide the knot under the button and prevent it from showing on the wrong side of the garment.

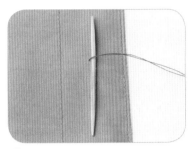

**4** Place a toothpick directly on the garment. Leave the toothpick there as you sew to create a space between the button and the fabric.

**5** Loop the needle and thread up one of the holes in the button and back down into the garment fabric. Sew only through the top layer of the fabric.

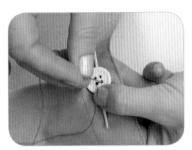

**6** Repeat step 5 three or four more times, then sew the other side of the button (if necessary) in the same manner until the button is secure.

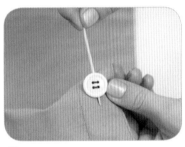

**7** Slip the toothpick out.

**8** Holding the button at the top of the thread loops created in steps 5 and 6, wrap the needle and thread under the button three or four times around, creating a thread shank.

**9** Catch the top garment fabric with the needle, and tie a knot in the thread.

**10** Put the needle in the top layer of fabric right beside the knot, and take it out 1" (2.5 cm) away from the knot.

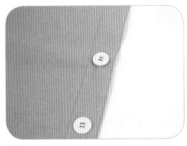

**11** Pull the thread tight so the knot pulls into the fabric, and trim the thread ends, which will now disappear into the fabric.

## TIP

Adding a thread shank creates a space between the button and fabric, and is especially important for thicker fabrics. When the button is closed, a shank prevents puckering and also reduces tugging and pulling at the button.

# MEND IT **UNRAVELING BUTTONHOLE**

Buttonholes experience wear and tear every time you do up or undo a button. And when a buttonhole undergoes repeated strain, the threads around it can break and eventually start to unravel.

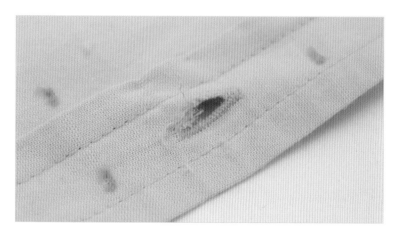

Once unraveling starts, it will continue, so it's advisable to fix it right away. To mend an unraveling buttonhole, you can either handsew or machine sew it. Both techniques can be used on numerous buttonhole types and fabrics.

## SOLUTION ONE: HANDSEW

1. Trim any spare threads and frayed fibers from around the edge of the buttonhole.

2. Double-thread a handsewing needle and tie a knot at the end. From the wrong side of the buttonhole, bring the needle through the fabric where the original buttonhole stitching is intact, and secure the knot of the new thread.

3. Loop the needle around the buttonhole back up to the right side of the fabric, and pull the threads tight.

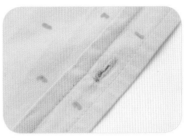

**TIP**
Be sure to match the new thread to the original buttonhole thread as best you can.

④ Repeat step 3 all the way around the unraveled area, keeping the stitches close together.

⑤ Tie a knot on the wrong side of the fabric and trim the thread ends.

## SOLUTION TWO: MACHINE SEW

① Trim any spare threads and frayed fibers from around the buttonhole.

② Set your machine to the zigzag stitch. Here, the pattern selector should be set to "C" for a zigzag.

③ Adjust the stitch width so it's mid-to-narrow. Here, the stitch width (the semi-dial on the top right side of the machine) is set to two out of five.

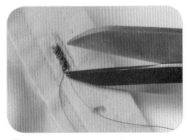

④ Shorten the stitch length to keep the stitches close together. On this machine, standard stitch length is 2.5, so for this repair, it's now at 1.

⑤ Sew over the unraveled thread using an overedge zigzag stitch. (Your needle will go on the fabric then off the fabric, encasing the raw edge with thread.)

⑥ Backstitch at the beginning and end of the stitch, and trim the thread ends.

# MEND IT **BROKEN CLASP**

Hearing the pop of your bra or swimsuit closure breaking can put a significant damper on your day. But while it may be an inconvenience, the garment is not a lost cause. Replacing a broken clasp can save both your garment and your day, and it's easy to do in just a few steps.

## SWIMWEAR AND LINGERIE HARDWARE

Different closures and hardware are readily available at your local sewing supply store or online. Here are some of the most common types of hardware for swimwear and lingerie:

- Clips: The pieces often used on straps to create a racerback
- Extenders: The closure with three sets of hook and eyes usually seen on the back of a bra
- Rings: The circular hardware that attaches a strap to the main garment
- S hooks (shown here): The closure usually seen on bikini tops
- Slides: Straps are threaded through slides to allow you to adjust the strap length.

# SOLUTION: REPLACE THE CLASP

① Using a seam ripper, carefully remove the stitches that are holding the clasp in place.

② Thread the strap through the new clasp the same way it was originally.

③ Pin the strap in place around the new clasp.

④ Topstitch along the original stitch line.

⑤ Backstitch at both ends and trim the threads.

⑥ For added strength and security, repeat steps 4 and 5 along the same stitch line.

## TIP

Swimsuits and bras are typically made of fabrics that can snag easily, so use extra caution when removing the existing clasp with a seam ripper.

# MEND IT **DETACHED BELT LOOP**

Belts and their fashionable-but-sometimes-cumbersome buckles can be quite heavy. This added weight can cause the belt loop on a garment to become detached from the waistline.

Not only is a detached belt loop useless but it also makes your garment look old and tired. There are two types of belt loops: a carrier (made of fabric and commonly seen on pants) and a chain loop (made of thread and mostly seen on delicate garments including dresses). Reattach a carrier with a simple stitch or make a new chain loop by hand.

## **SOLUTION ONE:** REATTACH THE CARRIER

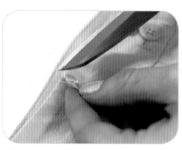

**1** Using a seam ripper or scissors, remove any stitches and loose threads from around the detached part of the carrier.

**2** Pin the detached carrier back in place, being sure to tuck under the raw edge.

**3** Double-thread a handsewing needle and tie a knot at the end. From the right side of the garment under the top fold of the carrier, enter the needle through the fabric to the wrong side in order to hide the knot.

4 Handsew across the top of the carrier (where the original stitching was) through all layers of the fabric.

5 From the garment wrong side, tie the thread in a knot and trim the ends. For a carrier that will hold a heavy belt, repeat step 4 for added security.

## TIP

Use a thicker thread when doing a chain loop so it can support the weight of a belt. Try an upholstery thread, depending on the weight of your fabric.

## SOLUTION TWO: MAKE A NEW CHAIN LOOP

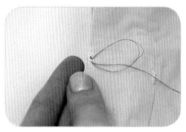

1 Using a seam ripper and scissors, remove the previous chain or belt loop from the garment, and mark the top and bottom points of the loop with a marking pencil.

2 At the top mark, pick up a few fibers of fabric and secure the knot of the thread.

3 Enter and exit the fabric again at the same point, and pull the thread until it forms a loop.

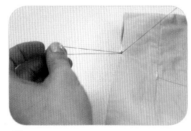

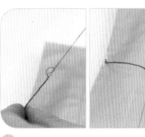

4 Reach your left hand (or the one without the needle) through the loop, and grab hold of the base of the thread.

5 While pulling the base of the thread back through the loop to your left, pull tight on the needle in the opposite direction, securing a slipknot. Repeat steps 3 and 4 continuously to create a replacement chain loop.

6 Tie a knot at the end of the chain loop once it's slightly longer than the distance between your marks in step 1 in order to accommodate a belt. Secure the chain loop to the bottom mark with a few stitches. From the garment wrong side, tie the thread in a knot and trim the ends.

# MEND IT **STRETCHED ELASTIC**

When it comes to elastic, time is not your friend. Elastic can deteriorate over time and lose its stretchiness with wear—every time your body moves, and every time your garment is put on and taken off.

When elastic wears out and loses its stretch, the best solution is to remove it and replace it with a new one.

## SOLUTION: REPLACE THE ELASTIC

1. To remove the old elastic from the inside of the garment, use a seam ripper to open up the casing about 2" (5 cm).

2. Cut the stretched elastic and pull it out of the casing.

3. Measure the desired length of the new elastic; add 1" (2.5 cm). As a general standard, for every 7" (18 cm) of your waist, subtract 1" (2.5 cm) to find the proper length for the new elastic.

4 Attach a safety pin to the end of the new elastic, and push the safety pin into the hole in the casing created in step 1.

5 Tunnel the elastic through the original casing by using the safety pin. Push the safety pin to the left, pinch the safety pin with your left hand, then smooth out the casing to the right.

6 Once the new elastic has gone all the way around the garment and back out the original entry point, remove the safety pin and overlap the elastic ends by ½" (1.3 cm).

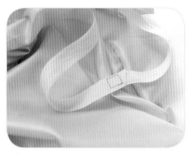

7 Stitch a box around the overlapped elastic to secure the ends.

8 Push the elastic all the way into the casing, and pin the casing closed.

9 Sew the casing closed by topstitching along the original stitch line, being sure to overlap any existing stitches on either end.

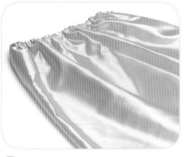

10 Backstitch at both ends of the stitch and trim the thread ends.

## TIPS

- Try to find elastic that is a similar weight and width as the original.
- When measuring the new elastic length, make sure that it's a comfortable fit for your body and for the use of the garment.

# MEND IT **BROKEN ZIPPER**

Vintage hunters know that there are some great finds out there. Unfortunately, some of those great finds come with a broken zipper.

Similarly, zippers on our everyday garments often either get stuck or the teeth break. But broken zippers can be replaced to give new life to your favorite piece or fabulous find.

### NAVIGATING AROUND ZIPPER

To navigate around the zipper pull, lower the needle into the fabric once you're at the zipper pull. Lift up the presser foot and move the pull out of the way by either opening or closing the zipper 1" (2.5 cm). Lower the presser foot and continue sewing.

## **SOLUTION:** REPLACE THE ZIPPER

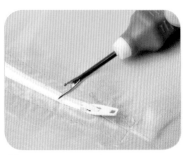

1 Using a seam ripper, remove the topstitching, the broken zipper, and any stray threads.

2 Place the right sides of the fabric together, matching up the original seam, and pin the fabric in place.

3 Baste the original seam closed, overlapping any existing stitches slightly. Backstitch at the beginning and end of the stitch, and trim the thread ends. (A baste is your longest stitch length.)

④ Press the seam flat, then open.

⑤ Place the zipper right-side down (teeth down) over the seam allowance. Line up the zipper bottom stop with the bottom of the baste stitch from step 3, and align the zipper teeth with the seam. Pin one side of the zipper tape to the seam allowance only (don't go through the garment fabric).

⑥ Switch the machine to a zipper foot, and unzip the zipper about 2" (5 cm).

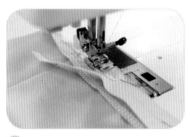

⑦ Baste the zipper tape to the seam allowance only, from the very top of the tape to the very bottom of the tape. To navigate around the zipper pull, see opposite.

⑧ Pin the other side of the zipper tape to the other seam allowance, and baste as in step 7.

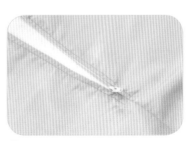

⑨ Flip the fabric over to the right side. Feel for the zipper bottom stop, and make a small mark just below it.

⑩ With a seam ripper, remove the baste stitches from the top 2" (5 cm) of the zipper, revealing the zipper teeth. Open the zipper 2" (5 cm).

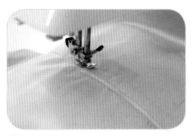

⑪ Topstitch a box around the zipper approximately ⅜" (1 cm) away from the seam, pivoting at the mark from step 9. Backstitch at both ends and trim the threads.

⑫ Remove the remaining baste stitches.

CLOSURES

# *Make it Fabulous*

## GO DECORATIVE

If you're looking to spice up a garment you've had for a while or if it's too simple for your taste, there's no easier way to get your style on than to change the buttons. Try replacing existing buttons with vintage or decorative ones—they'll make your garment go from basic to bold in an instant. Get creative by choosing contrasting buttons that show your personality and your flair for style.

▷ See Also: Add studs, page 26

1. Use scissors to cut the original button away from the garment.

2. Double-thread a handsewing needle, and tie a knot at the end.

3. From the right side of the fabric, secure the knot of the thread.

4. Loop the needle and thread through the hole in the shank of the new button, and back down into the garment fabric.

5. Repeat step 4 three or four times until the button is secure.

6. Tie a knot. Trim the thread ends.

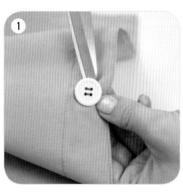

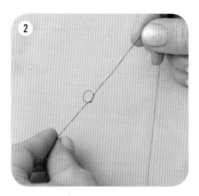

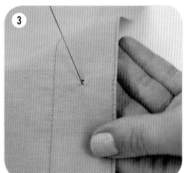

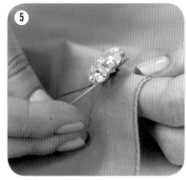

## Tip

Want to make sure your button doesn't budge? Coat the thread with wax before sewing. (For detailed instructions, see Missing button, page 90.)

Clockwise from left: Buttons handsewn by Jenna Richardson to floral skirt; Black and white gingham playsuit with pink buttons handmade by Quincy of Q's Daydream Etsy shop, featured on Claude Monique Viard's blog; Vintage white blazer with gold buttons and detailing featured on Chariot Marie's Etsy shop.

# *Make it Fabulous*

## CHANGE THE CLOSURE

No matter how chic your outfit may be, outdated or damaged closures are never in style. To ensure your garment is best-dressed, simply change the closure. Try swapping a standard zipper for buttons and loops or hook and eyes, or change a buttonhole into a frog closure as shown here. A new, unexpected closure will give your garment a stylish, updated look that will keep you wearing it for years to come.

▷ See Also: Change the shape, page 80; Change it out, page 122

1. Cut the button off the garment and use a seam ripper to remove the stitches around the buttonhole.

2. To stabilize the fabric at the hole, cut a piece of fusible interfacing that is ½" (1.3 cm) larger than the buttonhole on all sides.

3. With wrong sides together, secure the interfacing to the fabric at the hole by pressing and holding an iron over it for 5 to 10 seconds.

4. Pin the frog closure in place, covering the buttonhole with one side and the button placement with the other side.

5. Handsew the frog closure to the garment using a pick stitch. (For details, follow steps 2 to 5 on page 28).

6. Tie a knot on the wrong side of the fabric and trim the thread ends.

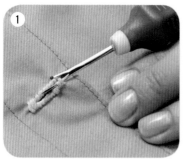

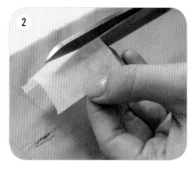

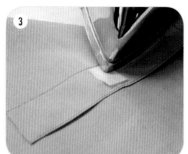

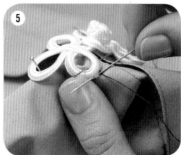

*Tip*

When choosing a new closure, take the weight of the fabric into consideration, and also evaluate how quickly or frequently the closure will be used.

Clockwise from left: Blue blazer from Romwe featured on Anastasia Siantar's blog; Dion Lee jacket with button detail skirt featured on Feed Me NaNa's blog; Embossed dress by Siren London featured on Mayo Wo's blog.

# *Make it Fabulous*

## ADD HARDWARE

Although belt loops are functional, they don't have to be boring. Try replacing your garment's original belt loops with chains or hardware. Hardware and metal accessories will add personal style with edge, and they're easy to sew in place.

▷ See Also: Add studs, page 26

1. Use a seam ripper to remove the original belt loop.

2. Cut a chain to the same length as the belt loop (without the seam allowance) using wire cutters.

3. Double-thread a handsewing needle and tie a knot at the end. From the wrong side of the fabric, secure the knot of the thread.

4. Pass the needle through the top link of the chain.

5. Loop the needle through the chain link and the fabric multiple times, pulling the thread tight. Tie a knot on the wrong side of the garment, and trim the thread ends.

6. Repeat steps 3 to 5 to attach the bottom link of the chain to the other side of the waistband.

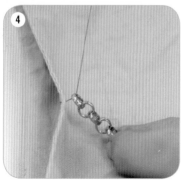

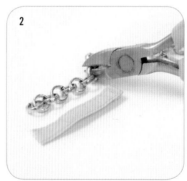

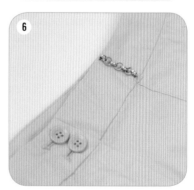

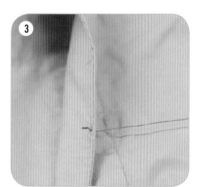

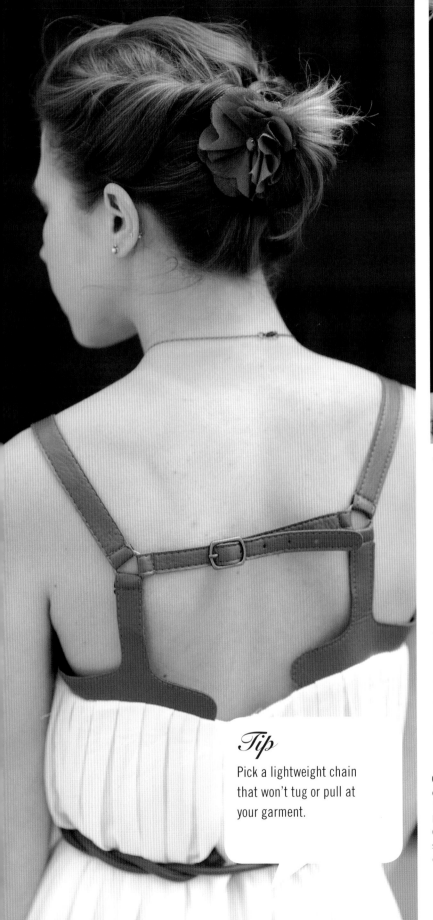

## Tip

Pick a lightweight chain that won't tug or pull at your garment.

Clockwise from left: Leather strap dress by Tailor and Stylist featured on Kayley Heeringa's blog; Vintage black blazer with gold clasps featured on Chariot Marie's Etsy shop; Short pencil skirt with wide band and metal zippers designed by Meisterkluft.

# *Make it Fabulous*

## BE BRIGHT

Sometimes the smallest changes can make a big difference. If you're looking to make a statement with a pop of color, simply change the thread of your buttonhole. You can use a contrasting embroidery thread around an existing buttonhole opening, or try a rayon thread, which has a bold, vibrant sheen.

▷ See Also: Go contrast, page 56

1. Remove any threads and frayed fibers from around the buttonhole.

2. Using a contrasting thread, double-thread a handsewing needle and tie a knot at the end. From the wrong side of the buttonhole, secure the knot of the new thread.

3. Loop the thread around the buttonhole, encasing the fabric raw edge.

4. Repeat step 3 down the entire side of the buttonhole, keeping the stitches close together.

5. At the narrow end of the buttonhole, sew a longer stitch to create a bartack. Repeat this twice in the same spot then continue down the other side of the buttonhole and repeat the bartacks at the other end.

6. Tie a knot on the wrong side of the garment. Trim the thread ends.

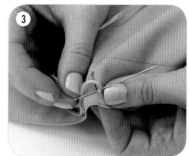

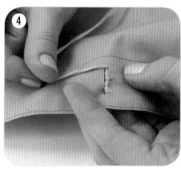

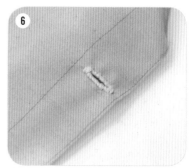

**Tip**

Be sure to remove all of the old thread from the original buttonhole first. This will prevent the new contrasting thread from making the finished buttonhole too thick.

Clockwise from left: Embellished buttonholes on H&M sweater worn by Rebecca Hawkins; Button detail on Boden sweater worn by Rebecca Hawkins; Gold button sweater by La Redoute.

# STRAPS

Clockwise from left: Printed dress by La Redoute; Leather strap dress by Tailor and Stylist featured on Kayley Heeringa's blog; Halter T-Bar top featured on Penelope's Wild Trim website.

STRAPS

# MEND IT **SEPARATED STRAP**

Spaghetti straps are so-called for their slenderness. And while spaghetti straps are fashionable, they're also weak because they are made from a minimal amount of fabric.

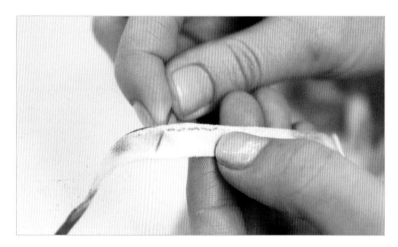

Threads on spaghetti straps can eventually tear or break from stress, causing the strap to separate along the side. However, they can easily be sewn back up either by hand or by machine.

## **SOLUTION ONE:** HANDSEW THE STRAP

① Trim any spare threads or frayed fibers from around the area.

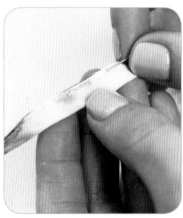

② Pin the separated strap closed.

③ Double-thread a handsewing needle and tie a knot at the end.

4 To hide the thread knot, push the needle from the inside of the strap, and bring it to the right side of the fabric.

5 Taking small stitches, sew the separated strap closed by weaving up and down through the fabric.

6 Tie a knot and trim the thread ends. To hide the knot and thread ends, follow steps 9 to 11 on page 73.

## SOLUTION TWO: MACHINE SEW THE STRAP

1 Trim any spare threads from around the tear.

2 Pin the separated strap closed.

3 Using a regular stitch, machine sew the separated strap closed. Overlap any existing stitches, and backstitch at both ends.

4 Trim the thread ends.

5 You can press the strap with an iron to set the stitches and to make them look polished.

**TIP**

When sewing a fabric that has multiple colors, choose a thread similar to the background or one that matches the most common color. A clear thread will be nearly invisible.

# MEND IT **BROKEN LINGERIE STRAP**

Lingerie straps play an important role: they're responsible for lifting and holding. Once a strap breaks, it can no longer fulfill its very important responsibilities.

But don't toss away your expensive foundation garments just because the strap is broken. The best solution (and the one that will avoid an unsightly bulge) is to replace the strap with a brand new one. Finding a similar elasticized strap to your original is key.

## SOLUTION: REPLACE THE STRAP

Using a seam ripper, remove the broken strap from the lingerie, and remove the hardware from the broken strap.

Measure the length of the original broken strap.

Cut the new elasticized strap to the length from step 2.

Thread the new strap through the lingerie's original hardware.

Follow the original path through the lingerie slider.

Pin the new strap in place at the top of your lingerie.

Sew along the original stitch line, backstitching at both ends and trimming the threads.

Continue threading all of the strap ends through the slider.

Sew the new strap at the slider, backstitching at both ends.

Trim the excess strap, then trim the thread ends.

Adjust the slider as needed to ensure a perfect fit.

## TIP

Sliders are the hardware that lingerie straps are threaded through, and they allow for easy strap length adjustment.

STRAPS

# MEND IT **BROKEN PURSE CHAIN**

Considering how much we carry in our purses everyday, it's a surprise that purse straps stay intact at all.

When your purse strap chain breaks, you might be tempted to throw it away. Instead, fix a broken chain strap by simply replacing it with a new one. No welding is required, but you'll need some needle-nose pliers.

**TIP**
Find a chain similar in weight and finish to the one that you're replacing or try something chunkier or finer to change the overall look of your bag.

# SOLUTION: REPLACE CHAIN

1. Use pliers to remove the old chain by carefully opening the last link.

2. Measure the length of the old chain.

3. Use wire cutters to cut the new chain to the length of the old chain.

4. Wrap the new chain around the bag's original hardware.

5. Use a set of needle-nose pliers to open up the last link of the new chain.

6. Ensure the chain is wrapped around the bag's original hardware when preparing to close the link.

7. Close the last link around another link of the chain, securing the new chain to the bag.

8. Repeat steps 4 to 7 on the other side of the bag.

9. Test the durability of the links and tighten them as necessary.

STRAPS

# *Make it Fabulous*

## GO STRAPLESS

Strapless is a great clothing option when the mercury starts to rise, whether it's a style (and weather) preference or because a strap has broken. Removing existing straps means you'll be taking away what holds the garment up, so you'll want to sew in a clear lingerie elastic that will help keep the garment up by itself. Depending on the fit, you may also want to add boning at the seams for extra stability, but not all garments will allow for this.

▷ See Also: Make it contrast, page 120; Change it out, page 122

1. Using a seam ripper, remove the existing straps from the garment.

2. Measure the circumference of the top of the garment, and cut a piece of clear lingerie elastic to that measurement.

3. Fold under the two cut ends of the elastic ½" (1.3 cm) each. Pin the elastic along the top inside edge of the garment, stretching the elastic slightly to make it fit.

4. From the wrong side of the garment, sew the elastic in place all the way around.

5. Use a stretch stitch or a three-step zigzag stitch (shown here), which will allow for some movement and stretch across the top of the garment.

6. Backstitch at the beginning and end of the stitch, and trim the threads.

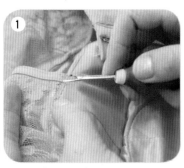

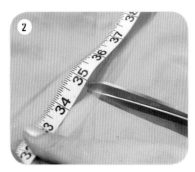

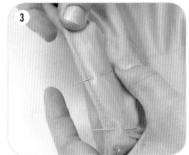

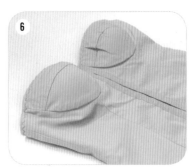

*Tip*

Clear lingerie elastic will grip
your skin to help keep the
garment in place.

Clockwise from left: Strapless romper
by Maisy Brown; Beatrice Taye in a
cotton strapless corset with yellow silk
lining designed by Solome Katongole;
Bustier by Pull & Bear featured on
Mayo Wo's blog.

STRAPS
# *Make it Fabulous*

## MAKE IT CONTRAST

Adding color to your wardrobe doesn't have to mean a shopping spree. You can make a statement with just a subtle pop of color. Switch out your existing straps with some in a contrasting tone. Have fun, and be creative!

▷ See Also: Go strapless, page 118; Change it out, page 122

1. Use a seam ripper to remove the straps from your garment, and also remove the hardware from the straps.

2. Cut new straps to the same length as the original straps.

3. Thread the new straps through the hardware the same way as the original straps.

4. Pin the new straps in place at the front and back of the garment.

5. Sew the new straps in place, backstitching at both ends.

6. Trim all of your threads.

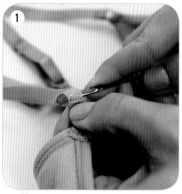

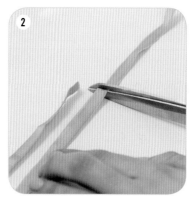

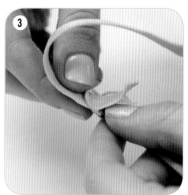

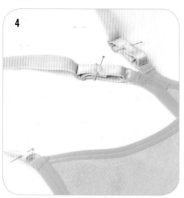

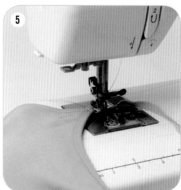

**Tip**

Try finding a new strap that is the same width and has a similar elasticity to the old strap.

Clockwise from left: Summer dress with black shoulder straps by Ralene van der Walt; Collar-back dress featured on Penelope's Wild Trim website; Graphite felt bag with brown natural leather straps handmade by Moose Design; Halter T-Bar top featured on Penelope's Wild Trim website.

# Make it Fabulous

## CHANGE IT OUT

Walk into any craft store and you will see aisles of colorful, fun, and fashionable ribbon. The exciting colors and patterns can bring new life to a garment with straps. Simply swap out the existing straps for ribbons to create a completely fresh and fashionable new look. Feel free to get creative and choose ribbons in patterns and textures that are outside the norm but do not choose ribbons that are too thin or wide for the garment.

▷ See Also: Go strapless, page 118; Make it contrast, page 120

1. Using a seam ripper, remove the straps from the garment.

2. Measure the length of the original strap, and double that measurement. Cut two pieces of ribbon to the new (doubled) length.

3. Pin the ribbon ends in the same place as the original straps at the front and the back of the garment, folding under the raw edges.

4. Topstitch along the original stitch line, backstitching at both ends and trimming the threads.

5. Cut the new strap ribbon pieces in half.

6. Try on the garment, and tie both ribbons in a bow at a suitable length.

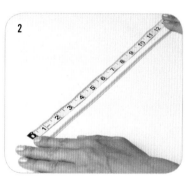
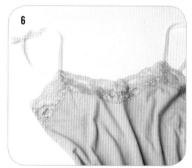

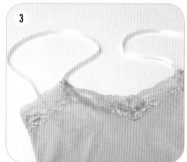

## Tip

If your ribbon is synthetic, hold the cut ends near a flame in order to melt them and prevent them from fraying.

Clockwise from left: Leanna dress by Hobbs; Hannah Smith in navy blue piping dress designed by Vivat Veritas; Leather strap dress by Tailor and Stylist featured on Kayley Heeringa's blog.

# COLOR

Clockwise from left: Button dress and floral scarf by EAST; Tevrow and Chase skirt and Costa Blanca jacket featured on My Edit blog; Ombre tights hand-dyed featured on BRZ's Etsy shop.

# MEND IT **FADED COLOR**

Time, wear, cleaning agents, and even ultraviolet rays all contribute to color fade in your garments. Fading is no cause for concern as long as you take action as soon as you notice the color beginning to soften. Bring your garment back to life by overdyeing it (dyeing over the existing color) for a bold and vibrant finished result.

### OVERDYEING

Bright, saturated tones and black hues will fade faster than other colors, and although almost every type of fabric (whether it's the thickest of wools or the thinnest of chiffons) is prone to fading, denim fabrics fade the fastest. Note that overdyeing—dyeing over an existing color—is different from dyeing, which is turning a white or cream fabric a completely different color. For a step-by-step tutorial on dyeing, see page 132.

# SOLUTION: OVERDYE

1 Using store-bought fabric dye, add the amount of salt indicated in the instructions to a container of hot water. Make sure you wear rubber gloves.

2 Add the correct amount of dye to the salt water and stir.

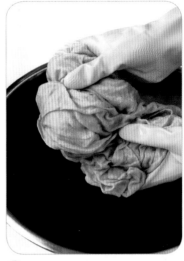

3 Wet your garment thoroughly before placing it into the dye solution.

4 Soak the garment in the dye, stirring it every few minutes. The longer you leave the garment in the dye, the darker the color will get.

5 Wring out the entire garment. To set the color, machine wash the dyed garment on its own in cold water, then tumble-dry it.

## TIPS

- Use liquid dye instead of powder for the most saturated, even results, and wash your garment before dying to remove any dirt or residue.
- Check the fabric content of your garment. Natural fibers, including silk and cotton, dye best, whereas blended fibers may need to be dyed a few times. Synthetic fabrics don't always take color well.

COLOR

# MEND IT **DISCOLORED VINTAGE FABRIC**

It seems as though vintage never goes out of style. However, if your vintage garments are stained, have yellowed, or lost their original color, they may end up looking old.

If the fabric of your vintage garment is discolored, you can revive it by either soaking it in a detergent containing enzymes or—if the garment was originally white—washing it in diluted bleach.

## KNOWING WHAT TO USE
If you know exactly what has discolored your vintage fabric, look for a detergent with an enzyme that will specifically target that problem since different

enzymes remedy different issues. For example, amylase removes starchy residues, lipase removes fatty and oily stains, protease removes protein stains, and cellulase removes particulate soils and brightens colors. If you have white vintage fabric, then bleach may be your answer, whether you're looking to remove stains or whiten overall.

## SOLUTION ONE: USE AN ENZYME DETERGENT

Pretreat the garment to remove dirt, residue, and superficial stains by washing it on its own in warm water.

Add a detergent containing enzymes to a bowl of water, following the directions on the instructions.

### TIP

Be careful not to get bleach on colored garments, and always rinse your washing machine with hot water after using bleach in order to remove any residue.

Soak the vintage fabric in the solution and let it stand—fully submerged in the enzyme detergent—for 5 to 10 minutes.

Wash the garment again in warm water (this time with no detergent), and repeat steps 2 and 3 if necessary.

## SOLUTION TWO: BLEACH IT

Pretreat the garment to remove dirt, residue, and superficial stains by washing it on its own in warm water.

Run the garment through the washing machine again, this time adding ⅛ cup (2 tbsp or 30 ml) of bleach in the designated area 5 minutes into the wash cycle.

Wash the garment again a final time in warm water (this time with no bleach), and repeat step 2 if necessary.

COLOR
## *Make it Fabulous*

## DIP DYE

Ombre—colors becoming progressively darker or lighter—is a popular color trend that can be seen all the way from the runway to the fashion blogs to the street. To get the look at home, whether you're covering a color flaw or just adding interest to a garment, it's easy to DIY dip dye. Dip dyeing is the process of dipping a specific area of fabric into the dye, rather than submerging the entire garment.

▷ See Also: Dye new color, page 132; Fade and distress, page 134

To prepare your garment for dip dyeing, wash it on its own in warm water to remove dirt, residue, and superficial stains. Follow steps 1 to 3 from page 126 before continuing.

1. Dip just the portion of fabric you want to dye (usually the bottom or top of a garment) into the dye solution a few times.

2. Dip the garment in a separate container filled with cold water in order to set the color. Then wring the garment out.

3. Add more dye to the solution and repeat step 1, but dip about a third less of the fabric than you did previously in order to create an ombre effect.

4. Dip the garment again in a separate container filled with cold water in order to set the color. Wring the garment out.

5. Repeat steps 3 and 4, making sure you leave another one third of the garment out of the dye solution.

6. To set the color, machine wash the dyed garment on its own in cold water, then tumble dry it.

*Tip*

The longer you leave fabric in the dye solution, the darker the color will become.

Clockwise from left: Dip-dyed T-shirt by Jenna Richardson; Dip-dyed jumper from Eleven's A/W thirteen Collection by Ellie Rhodes; Tassel skirt from Lily Jean, cropped tank top from H&M featured on Anastasia Siantar's blog.

COLOR

# *Make it Fabulous*

## DYE NEW COLOR

If you have a garment that's out of season or looks uninspiring, dyeing it a new color can bring it back to life and even make it feel like a brand-new piece. Dyeing is the process of adding color to a white or ivory garment, which is not to be confused with overdyeing—dyeing a fabric that already has an existing color.

▷ See Also: Dip dye, page 130

1. Pretreat the garment to remove dirt, residue, and superficial stains by washing it on its own in warm water.

2. Place the wet garment in the basin of a front-load washing machine

3. Dissolve the dye in four cups of very hot tap water.

4. Set the machine for its extended wash cycle in order to keep the fabric immersed in dye for at least 30 minutes.

5. Pour the dissolved dye into the machine's detergent dispenser, followed by four cups of very hot tap water in order to clean the dispenser.

6. Once the wash cycle is complete, dry the garment in the dryer to set the color.

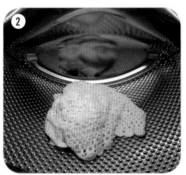

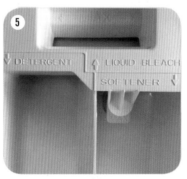

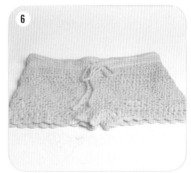

## Tips

- Be sure to follow the instructions that come with your dye in case the steps differ from one brand or dye type to the next.
- To make the finished color darker, add a touch of black dye to any colored dye. And to make a finished color lighter, dilute the dye mixture with water.

Ivory cable knit cardigan and silk red dress by La Redoute.

COLOR

*Make it Fabulous*

## FADE AND DISTRESS

If your garment has a stain or another type of color flaw, turn it into a stylish design detail by fading and distressing the discoloration. Garments with intentional fading and distressing have been in style for many years, and fading them or distressing them yourself is very easy to do. Although you can fade and distress fabric anywhere, it's best to do it where your garment would naturally experience the most wear and tear, such as the collar, elbow, thigh, knee, or hem.

▷ See Also: Bleach it, page 136

1. Wash the garment in very hot water several times to wear down the fabric fibers and make fading and distressing easier.

2. Lay the garment flat and use a rough-grade sandpaper to rub the area you wish to fade until you reach the desired color. Rub gently, checking every few rubs to ensure you don't damage the fabric.

3. Repeat the process as necessary in different areas, depending on the look you're going for.

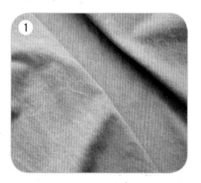

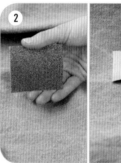

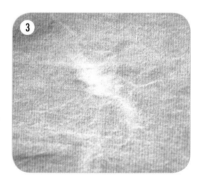

*Tips*

- Fading works best on durable woven fabrics such as denim and cotton twill. Never try fading and distressing a knit garment—knit fabrics will pill and the garment will be ruined.
- Fading and distressing fabric is permanent, so start small and increase the size (or add additional faded areas for style) once you're comfortable with the technique.

Clockwise from left: Vintage blazer, and American Eagle T-shirt featured on Veronica Popoiacu's blog; Nasty Gal croptop and Minkpink shorts as featured on Cindy Chi's blog; Blazer and jeans by Gap featured on Kayley Heeringa's blog.

COLOR
## *Make it Fabulous*

## BLEACH IT

Instead of tossing away a garment that's been flawed with a stain or another type of discoloration, take the opportunity to get creative. Bleach can be strategically used to create a design or pattern while removing a fabric discoloration at the same time. Use a bleach pen to remove your garment's color in a specific spot, either replicating a design you love or customizing your own pattern.

▷ See Also: Fade and distress, page 134

1. Pretreat the garment to remove dirt, residue, and superficial stains by washing it on its own in warm water.

2. Lay the garment flat and slide a piece of wax paper underneath the top layer of fabric to prevent bleach from going through to the bottom layer.

3. Draw the design for the bleach directly on the fabric with a marking pencil.

4. Test the bleach pen on a paper towel to make sure it isn't clogged, and that the bleach comes out smoothly.

5. Trace over your chalk design with the bleach pen, and leave the bleach on the garment until the fabric color dissipates. (This could take 15 to 30 minutes, but it really depends on your fabric, so keep a close eye on it.)

6. To set the design and remove excess bleach, machine wash the garment on its own in warm water.

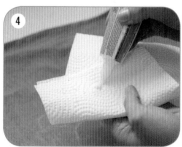

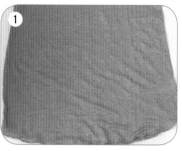

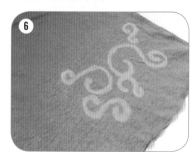

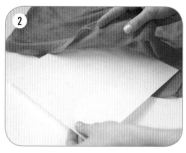

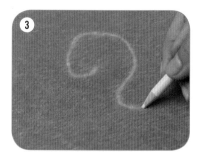

> **Tip**
>
> Keep your design simple to prevent the bleach from running. Lines, dots, and basic shapes work best.

Clockwise from left: Bleached denim shorts by Jenna Richardson; Tribal print added to WetSeal leggings with a bleach pen by Reese Kistel; Leah McIntosh in bleached, splattered American Eagle dress by Julie Ann Art.

# GARMENT CARE

Clockwise from left: Vintage blue ruffle dress with brown belt featured in Chariot Marie's Etsy shop; Sheer top by Laurustinus and faux-leather diamond pleated skirt by Chicwish featured on Mayo Wo's blog; Sailboat print lace-back midi dress designed by Lowie.

GARMENT CARE
# LAUNDERING

Proper laundering plays an important role in keeping your wardrobe looking luxe. Here are some general laundering tips that are easy to implement and will help ensure the long life of your garments.

- Before washing a garment, check it for any repairs that are needed. Tears, loose threads, and fallen hems should be dealt with before laundering in order to prevent the flaw from becoming bigger.

- For the best results, always follow your garment's washing instructions on the care label.

- Trust a professional dry cleaner to handle leather and suede, delicate fabrics, heavily soiled garments, and garments that have a significant number of embellishments such as beads and sequins.

- Heat, agitation, sun, and sometimes even water can wear out fabric fibers. Because of this, you should launder garments carefully and only when necessary.

- Turn your dark and heavily saturated colored clothing inside out to prevent the colors from fading. Do the same with any embellished garments to prevent the embellishments from snagging or falling off.

- Do up the zippers on your garments before washing them to prevent the zipper teeth from catching and pulling other clothing.

- Wash garments of the same outfit together in the same manner (for example, dry-clean a jacket and matching skirt) in order to keep the colors fading and fibers wearing at the same rate.

- To keep distortion, fiber wear, and color loss to a minimum, it's best to wash all of your garments in cold water and to either lay them flat to dry or hang them.

- In general, choose cold water for bold, bright colors and blacks, as well as fabrics that might shrink. Warm water is suitable for light to medium colors, as well as fabrics that won't shrink and are blended with 50% polyester. Hot water is suitable for whites, towels and bedding, and baby items.

- If you're using a dryer, choose the "automatic dry" setting, which stops the cycle when your clothes are dry, ensuring your garments aren't exposed to excess heat in a longer-than-needed dry cycle.

Opposite: Watta Bundor in an orange-dotted one-shoulder peplum shirt designed by Solome Katongole.

# FABRIC CARE BY TYPE

When laundering your favorite pieces, it's best to follow the care symbols on the garment tag. Just as textiles vary in their properties, they also need to be cared for in their own way. Here are some detailed care instructions based on fabric type.

## ACRYLIC

Machine-wash acrylic fabric with warm water, and use a fabric softener to keep static electricity at bay. You can tumble-dry your acrylic garments, but pull them out of the dryer while they're still slightly damp and hang them up to finish drying in order to prevent wrinkling.

## ALPACA

Alpaca is a stronger fiber than wool, but it should still be cared for very carefully. Dry-clean your alpaca garments and accessories, or handwash them with care. (Check the fabric care label for specific guidance.)

## ANGORA

Angora fibers are extremely fragile, so it's important that you handwash them with care. Use a light touch when washing, and don't wring or squeeze the garments. After washing, remove the water by putting your angora garment through the washing machine's spin cycle. Then lay it flat to dry.

## CASHMERE

Handwash cashmere garments in warm water, and use a mild shampoo as a detergent. Dissolve a capful of shampoo in water before adding the garment, then rinse the cashmere with hair conditioner for softness.

## COTTON

Wash cotton garments in warm or cold water, and tumble-dry them on low to medium heat. Be cautious of fiber distortion—cottons that haven't been pretreated will shrink when laundered, especially if you use hot water and a hot dryer; shrinkage can sometimes even occur when using warm water.

## FAUX FUR

It's best to take your faux fur garments to a dry-cleaner, although check the care label in case yours can be cared for at home. Fill a top-load washing machine with cold water, setting it for a medium-size load. Add a mild, color-safe detergent to the water, then add your faux fur. Let it soak in the water for 15 minutes with no agitation. Set the machine to drain and spin. Fill the machine again with cold water and let it drain and spin again. Make sure the machine never agitates the faux fur but only spins it dry. Hang the faux fur over a shower-curtain rod for one to two days, moving it often to prevent marks from appearing.

## FUR

Fur garments that undergo a lot of wear should be taken to a professional furrier annually to be cleaned.

## KNITTED GARMENTS

Knitted garments should be handwashed in lukewarm water with a mild soap. Don't wring them and don't agitate them too much; instead, just squeeze them gently before rinsing them thoroughly. Reshape the knitted garment while you lay it flat to dry.

## LACE

Handwash delicate lace in cold water using a mild detergent. More durable items can be machine-washed in a netted lingerie bag on a delicate cycle. Roll your lace in a towel to absorb excess water, then lay it flat to dry, reshaping as needed.

## LEATHER

Care for your leather garments with a leather conditioner and protector once or twice per year, depending on wear. You can carefully spot-treat small areas with a leather cleaner and a damp cloth, but for anything more significant, take your leather garment to a dry cleaner that specializes in leather care.

## LINEN

Check your garment's care instructions, as most linens should be dry-cleaned. If your linen garment can be machine-washed, use a mild detergent plus a fabric softener, and choose a short, delicate setting with minimal agitation. Reshape the linen garment while you lay it flat to dry.

## METALLIC FABRIC

Check the care label of your garments made with metallic fabric. If the garment can be washed, be sure to use cold water, and lay the garment flat to dry.

## NYLON

Nylon garments can be washed in warm water both by hand and also in a washing machine using a delicate cycle. Add fabric softener to reduce static electricity.

## POLYESTER

Polyester is a resilient fabric that can be machine-washed in warm water. Use a fabric softener to reduce static, and tumble-dry or lay flat to dry, depending on the delicacy of your garment.

## RAYON

Check your garment-care label because most rayon garments are damaged by water and should only be dry-cleaned. Those that can be washed should be cleaned by hand or on a delicate machine cycle (in a netted bag) in cold water, using a mild detergent. Don't wring or twist a rayon garment. Lay it flat to dry.

## SILK

Most silk garments should be dry-cleaned, but check the garment-care label. Silk that can be washed should be handwashed only in cool water using a mild detergent or baby soap. Don't agitate, wring, or twist silk; instead, gently swirl the garment through soapy water. Rinse it carefully, then blot the silk garment with a towel to absorb excess water before laying it flat to dry.

## SPANDEX

Hand- or machine-wash Spandex in warm water, and don't use any chlorine bleach. Hang your Spandex garments to dry or tumble-dry them on a low heat setting.

## SUEDE

Use a suede brush to gently dust dirt and debris off your suede accessories, and to keep the suede texture in its best condition. If your suede has stains or needs a more thorough cleaning, take it to a dry cleaner that specializes in suede care.

## SYNTHETIC FIBERS

Handwash synthetic fibers or use a gentle cycle on the washing machine. Tumble-dry them on a very low setting, and when ironing, be sure to use the synthetic setting. It's best to test a corner of your garment or a swatch of the synthetic fabric first, since many (including acetate) often distort when they come in contact with water or even heat.

## VELVET

Check your garment's care instructions to see if the velvet needs to be dry-cleaned. Velvet garments that can be washed at home can be handwashed with minimal agitation, then hung to dry or laid flat carefully so they don't crush. You can also brush the velvet (in one direction) with a fabric brush or cloth, steam it, then brush it again.

## WOOL

Most wool garments should be dry-cleaned, so check your garment's care label. Those that can be washed at home should be gently handwashed in cool water using a mild detergent. Don't rub, wring, or twist the garment; instead squeeze it loosely and carefully. Roll your wool garment in a towel to absorb excess water before reshaping it and laying it flat to dry.

Opposite: Skirt by Shona Roon for her blog.

# TOOLS USED IN THIS BOOK

**Bleach pen**
Look for a specially designed writing utensil that allows you to apply bleach onto fabric precisely.

**Bowl**
A large, non-porous container with a wide opening is useful when dyeing and bleaching fabrics.

**Enzyme detergent**
A soap alternative that helps remove stains, refresh discoloration, brighten whites, and revive vintage fabrics.

**Candle, taper**
When you draw your thread across this alternative to sewing beeswax, you'll strengthen it and prevent it from tangling—perfect for hand-sewing and attaching buttons.

**Flexible tape measure**
A flexible tape measure is a sewing essential. This measuring tool will be used many times throughout each project from start to finish. Look for one made of fiberglass so it won't stretch over time, or look for one that's retractable for convenience.

**Fray block or fray stop**
This washable, flexible fabric glue helps prevent individual threads from fraying. It can be used on the raw edges of small fabric tears as well as on the end of serged seams.

**French curve**
This dressmaking ruler features a multitude of curves from gentle to sharp and can be used for easily creating or duplicating lines that aren't straight.

**Handsewing needle**
A sharp, sturdy sewing needle is an essential tool for any hand repairs.

**Iron**
Pressing is just as important as sewing when it comes to a professional-looking finished garment. An iron is also needed for applying fusible interfacing and iron-on embellishments. It's a good idea to have an ironing board on-hand—you'll need a sturdy surface to press on.

**Marking pencil**
This fabric-friendly colored pencil (it washes out) is an alternative to tailor's chalk, and is used to mark fabric.

**Pin cushion**
A pin cushion holds your pins and keep them in one place. The tomato pin cushion is the most common, but you'll also find various decorative shapes, wrist pin cushions, and magnetic pin cushions.

**Piping and cording foot**
This sewing machine presser foot is specifically designed for sewing piping or cord in place; however, because it's so narrow and because it can be finely adjusted into position, it's also suitable for sewing zippers in place (both invisible and regular).

**Pliers**
A good quality pair of pliers is essential for working with hardware including chains, and will help you easily open and close hooks, links, and closures.

Opposite: Photography by Sherry Heck.

### Sand paper

A rough, medium-grade sandpaper can be used to break down fabric fibers in order to create the look of wear, distress, and discoloration.

### Scissors, fabric

Scissors that are used to cut fabric should never be used to cut anything else. Keep your fabric scissors labeled and hidden to prevent accidental use on things like paper and plastic.

### Sewing machine

Although it's not essential for all of the ideas in this book, a sewing machine is a great investment. You can use it to sew a new wardrobe from scratch, and it can help make many repairs much simpler and quicker.

### Straight pins

Straight dressmaking pins are necessary to hold fabric to fabric and also to hold paper, tissue, or embellishments in place.

### Thread

The proper thread is key for any sewing project, and you want to make sure it's the very best quality. Avoid threads that are old or used since time, light, and heat can cause thread fibers to weaken. And have a variety of threads on-hand, always making sure you have enough thread before you start a project.

### Toothpick

A plain toothpick might not seem like a typical sewing tool, but it's an essential tool for creating a shank when sewing on a button.

### Washing machine

A standard washing machine helps prep and set garments when you're enhancing and manipulating colors.

### Wire cutters

It's good to have a small pair of wire cutters on hand when working with chain or other hardware.

# GLOSSARY

·····························································································

### ALTERATION
An adjustment, change, or modification made to a garment or a pattern to improve the overall fit of the finished garment.

### BACKSTITCH OR BACKTACK
A type of stitch that is created by sewing backward over the top of existing stitches at the start or end of a line of stitching in order to prevent unraveling.

### BASTING STITCH
A method of temporarily joining fabric, either by hand or by machine, using a long stitch and no backstitch to make it easier to remove. This technique is most commonly used for fitting zippers, and to secure slippery or difficult fabrics while sewing.

### BIAS GRAIN See Grain

### BIAS TAPE OR BIAS BINDING
Long strips of fabric cut on the bias, used to finish the raw edge of a hem or a seam, especially for curved areas like neck and armholes. Bias tape can either be bought prepackaged or made from coordinating or matching fabrics.

### BLIND HEM STITCH
A virtually invisible hemming technique in which small zigzag stitches are made by hand between the hem and the garment. This technique can also be done by machine using the blind stitch setting.

### BOBBIN
The small plastic or metal spool that holds thread for the underside of the stitch in a sewing machine.

### BODICE
The portion of a pattern or a garment that runs from the shoulder to the waist.

### CROSSWISE GRAIN See Grain

### DART
A triangular or diamond-shaped mark on a pattern that, when folded and stitched, helps to shape a flat piece of fabric to the curves of the body. Darts are commonly used on the bust, waist, and hip.

### EASE
A method used to make a larger piece of fabric fit onto a smaller piece, through an even distribution of the extra fabric, avoiding gathers or tucks. The term "ease" can also refer to the difference between garment measurements and body measurements.

### EDGE STITCH
A row of straight stitching appearing $1/8$" (3 mm) from the edge of the fabric or garment, on the right side of the fabric, and through seam allowances. This technique is often used on cuffs and collars.

### FACING
Fabric, frequently with interfacing, applied on the inside of a sleeve, neck, or waist opening to finish and reinforce that opening.

### FEED DOGS
The parallel set of moving teeth below the needle and presser foot on a sewing machine. This part of the machine helps to grip and move the fabric along while sewing.

### FINGER PRESS
A method of temporarily flattening a seam so that it can be pressed more easily with an iron.

## FUSIBLE INTERFACING
See Interfacing

## FUSING
The action of bonding two layers of fabric together using a hot iron and a fusible material, which melts into glue.

## GATHERING
The process of drawing a fabric into a predetermined, smaller area, along a stitch line, to create soft folds.

## GRADING
The process of trimming a seam allowance to reduce bulk. This helps allow seams to lay flat and garments to hang properly, especially if facing and/or lining has been used. To grade a pattern also means to increase or decrease the size of a pattern, while maintaining the original proportion of that pattern.

## GRAIN
The direction in which fabric threads run. There are three types of grain: lengthwise, crosswise, and bias grain. Depending on the grain according to which the fabric is cut, the fabric will hang and behave differently. For example, fabric cut on a bias will be more stretchy than fabric cut on the lengthwise or crosswise grain.

**Bias grain** runs diagonally across the fabric, with a true bias running at a 45-degree angle to the selvedge of the fabric.

**Crosswise grain** runs perpendicular to the selvedge of the fabric.

**Lengthwise grain** runs parallel to the selvedge of the fabric.

## HAM, TAILOR'S
A hard form, resembling an actual ham, that is used to assist in the pressing of curves.

## HEM
The finished edge of a project, like the bottom of a skirt or sleeve, usually made by folding the edge under so that it is even, and securing it in place.

## INTERFACING
Specific type of fabric sewn or fused to the wrong side of a garment to stiffen, strengthen, or hold structure. Interfacing is commonly required in collars, cuffs, and waistbands, and is also useful in achieving structure in handbags and totes. It is available in a selection of weights, from ultra-light to heavy duty, and in fusible, sew-in, woven, and nonwoven varieties.

**Fusible interfacing**
Refers to interfacing with heat-activated glue on one side. It is quick, easy, and helps to prevent fraying, but tends to make the fabric crisper and more rigid than the sew-in variety. It also requires high heat to fuse, which may harm delicate fabrics.

**Sew-in interfacing** does not have any glue on the backside and must be sewn into the garment. Both glue-in and sew-in interfacing come in woven and nonwoven varieties:

**Nonwoven interfacing** refers to interfacing that is made by pressing fibers together, so that the interfacing appears paper-like.

**Woven interfacing** refers to fabric-like interfacing.

## KNITTED FABRIC
Fabric that has been made from yarn and constructed of consecutive rows of interlocking loops, like jersey.

## LENGTHWISE GRAIN See Grain

## LINING
An interior layer of fabric that is sewn into a garment, accessory, or bag that provides body and conceals construction details.

## MARKING

The process of transferring symbols from the paper pattern onto the fabric with chalk or tracing paper.

## NAP

A one-way direction of texture, such as velvet, or a one-way design, on the right side of a fabric. Fabrics with nap appear different when viewed from another direction, such as upside down.

## NONWOVEN FABRIC

Fabric that has been made by bonding fibers together mechanically, thermally, or chemically, like felt.

## NONWOVEN INTERFACING See Interfacing

## NOTCHES

The triangular marks on the cutting line of a pattern. When transferred to fabric, notches are used to align pieces that will be sewn together, and to help identify the front of the garment from the back.

## NOTIONS

The supplies beyond fabric that are required for completing a pattern or project, such as thread, buttons, or snaps. Commercial patterns usually list notions on the back of the pattern envelope.

## ON-GRAIN

When the lengthwise and crosswise threads are perpendicular to one another, or at right angles, the fabric is on-grain. Ensuring that fabric is on-grain is an important step in the processes to prepare fabric for cutting.

## OVERCAST/OVEREDGE ZIGZAG

This seam finish is a zigzag stitch that goes over the raw edge of fabric to prevent unraveling. See **Zigzag finish** for a slight variant of this seam finish.

## PINK

A type of seam finish that is achieved by trimming the raw edge of the seam allowance with pinking shears. This type of seam finish is best reserved for bulky fabrics that tend not to fray.

## PINKING SHEARS

A type of scissor with sawtooth blades, as opposed to straight, which leaves a zigzag pattern on cut fabric. Pinking shears are commonly used for decorative purposes and to prevent fabric from unraveling.

## PIVOT

The technique of turning a piece of fabric with the presser foot up and the needle down. Pivoting is often used to achieve a crisp corner while sewing.

## POINT PRESSER AND POUNDER

Used for pressing seams and corners and for pounding stubborn or thick fabrics flat.

## POINT TURNER AND CREASER

Used to help make points, corners, and creases crisp.

## PRESSER FOOT

A changeable sewing machine accessory that stabilizes the fabric and helps to feed it along while stitching. There are many different kinds of feet for different kinds of stitches and tasks. Common feet include the zigzag foot and the zipper foot.

## PRESSING

Using a hot iron on fabric. Pressing is most commonly used to smooth out wrinkles, to create defined folds in fabric, and to make a seam crisp.

## PRESSING CLOTH

A thin piece of fabric, similar in weight to a pillowcase, used when pressing to help prevent delicate fabrics from scorching, and to achieve crisper seams.

## RAW EDGE

The unfinished edge of fabric or the cut edge of a garment piece that may fray or unravel if left unfinished.

## REGULAR STITCH

Refers to a stitch created using the standard stitch length, 2.5, a backstitch at both ends, and a standard ⅝" (1.5 cm) seam allowance.

## RIGHT SIDE

The correct side of a piece of fabric, or the side of fabric intended to be seen in the finished product.

## SEAM

The line where separate pieces of fabric are joined and stitched together.

## SEAM ALLOWANCE

The area of fabric between the seam stitching and the cut edge.  Standard seam allowance is ⅝" (1.5 cm).

## SEAM FINISH

The technique used to prevent the raw edge of a seam allowance from unraveling. Common methods include overcasting, pinking, serging, and zigzagging.

## SEAM POUNDING

Using a smooth, blunt object to pound down bulk in a seam. Seam pounding is normally used to make bulky seams easier to stitch down, either by hand or with a sewing machine.

## SEAM RIPPER

A tool used for opening seams or unpicking stitches.

## SELVEDGE (also known as selvage)

The narrow, tightly woven border of the fabric, which is finished by the manufacturer and does not fray.

## SERGING

A type of seam finish found in professional garments that encloses the raw edge of a seam allowance in a thread casing and trims to a neat, consistent edge in one step. Also called overlocking.

## SEW-IN INTERFACING See Interfacing

## SEWING GAUGE

A small, metal ruler used to measure short distances with the aid of a sliding indicator for repeated measurements.

## SLEEVE BOARD

A small ironing board used for pressing narrow areas such as sleeves.

## SLEEVE ROLL

A smaller, more portable version of the sleeve board.

## SPOOL

A cylinder or cone that holds thread.

## STAYSTITCH

A stitch with short stitch length made inside the seam allowance, through a single thickness of fabric, to stabilize curved or slanted edges. These stitches are made before construction, backstitched at both ends, and are ⅛" (3 mm) from the fabric edge.

## STITCH IN THE DITCH

A type of stitch made on the right side of a garment, within the seam, that catches facing on the other side. This stitch is commonly used to sew on a waistband.

## STITCH LENGTH

How much fabric is fed under the presser foot for each stitch. For example, when the stitch length is decreased, less fabric will be fed under the presser foot, and when the stitch length is increased, more fabric will be fed under the presser foot, which results in a shorter or longer stitch length, respectively. Stitch length, in addition to tension, is adjusted according to the type of fabric being sewn, with standard stitch length being 2.5.

## STITCH WIDTH

The size of a stitch in the side-to-side direction. The stitch width setting is commonly used to achieve the desired width of a zigzag stitch. For example, when the stitch width is decreased, the width of the zigzag will be compressed; when it is increased, the width of the zigzag will be stretched, resulting in a narrower or wider zigzag, respectively.

## TACK

A temporary stitch used to hold fabric pieces together, usually removed after final stitching.

## TAILOR'S CHALK

A chalk pencil or chip used to mark fabric. Tailor's chalk is also called a "marking pen" or "marking pencil."

## TENSION

The amount of pull on the needle or bobbin thread. The tension is usually adjustable by dials on a sewing machine to accommodate different weights of fabrics, threads, and stitches.

## TEST SEAM

Stitching on a scrap of fabric to test the thread type, stitch type, stitch length, and tension used for a project.

## TOPSTITCH

A line of decorative or functional stitching on the fabric right side, 3/8" (1 cm) from the fabric edge.

## TRACING PAPER

A type of paper with chalk on one side, used with a tracing wheel to transfer markings from a pattern onto fabric.

## TRACING WHEEL

A small, pizza cutter-like tool used in conjunction with tracing paper to transfer markings from a pattern onto fabric.

## WOVEN FABRICS

Fabric that has been made by weaving threads together in the lengthwise and crosswise direction, like cotton and linen.

## WOVEN INTERFACING See Interfacing

## WRONG SIDE

The backside of the fabric, or, the side of fabric that is not intended to be seen in the finished product.

## ZIGZAG FINISH

A zigzag stitch that runs down the center of a seam allowance, which, once the excess is trimmed, prevents unraveling.

## ZIGZAG FOOT

A common type of presser foot that accommodates for the side-to-side motion of the needle during the zigzag stitch.

## ZIGZAG STITCH

A side-to-side stitch, that forms the letter Z, commonly used for finishing a seam, making buttonholes, and sewing stretch fabrics.

## ZIPPER FOOT

A common type of presser foot used to put in a zipper, which allows the needle to sew as close as possible to the zipper teeth.

# SUPPLIES

## DECORATIVE TRIMS

**M&J Trimming**
www.mjtrim.com

**Mokuba**
www.mokubany.com

**Pacific Trimming**
www.pacifictrimming.com

## FABRIC

**Camelot Fabrics**
www.camelotfabrics.com

**Fabricana**
www.fabricana.com

**JoAnn Fabric and Craft Stores**
www.joann.com

**Paron Fabrics**
www.manhattanfabrics.com

**Tonic Living**
www.tonicliving.com

## LINGERIE HARDWARE

**Bra Essentials**
www.braessentials.com

**Sew Sassy Fabrics**
www.sewsassy.com

## NOTIONS AND TOOLS

**Cansew**
www.cansew.com

**Steinlauf and Stoller**
www.steinlaufandstoller.com

**Stitch Craft Create**
www.stitchcraftcreate.co.uk

## PATTERNS

**BurdaStyle**
www.burdastyle.com

**The McCall Pattern Company**
www.mccall.com

**Simplicity**
www.simplicity.com

## SEWING INFORMATION AND EDUCATION

**LoveSewing**
www.lovesewing.com

**Sew Daily**
www.sewdaily.com

**Sewing Pattern Review**
www.patternreview.com

**The Sewing Studio**
www.lovesewingnewyork.com

# CONTRIBUTOR INDEX

With special thanks to:
EAST
Eucalyptus
Hobbs
Jenna Richardson
Kaliko
La Redoute
Rebecca Hawkins

# IMAGE CREDITS

Pg 6: Kristen Booth

Pg 8: Matthew Miller

Pg 9 T: Natalie Wong

Pg 9 B: Kyle Wong

Pg 25 TL &TR: Esther Coenen

Pg 25 CR: Mark Molloy

Pg 25 BL: Hannah Koelmeyer

pg 25 BR: Anna

Pg 27 TL: Heidi Adnum

Pg 27 TR: Volker Pietsch

Pg 27 BL: Kyle Wong

Pg 27 BR: Yessica Moline

Pg 29 L: Eric Sloan

Pg 29 TR & BR: Kyle Wong

Pg 31 T: Natalie Wong

Pg 31 BL: Miranda Anderson

Pg 31 BR: Anna Marie Cooper

Pg 32: Austin Reed

Pg 33 T: Scott Roon

Pg 33 B: Paul Hance

Pg 45 L: Jon Packard

Pg 45 R: Natascha Zivadinovic

Pg 47 L: Eunice Ng

Pg 47 TR: Anna

Pg 47 BR: Orlando Ricardo Ardana

Pg 48: Eucalyptus Clothing

Pg 49 T: Kaliko

Pg 49 B: La Redoute

Pg 57 L & TR: James Richardson

Pg 57 BR: Lucy Smith

Pg 59 TL: Kyle Wong

Pg 59 R: Natascha Zivadinovic

Pg 59 BL: Mandy Pellegrim

Pg 60: La Redoute

Pg 61 T: Kyle Wong

Pg 61 B: Kristen Booth

Pg 81 L: Kyle Wong

Pg 81 TR: Kristen Booth

Pg 81 BR: Eric Sloan

Pg 83 TL: Volker Pietsch

Pg 83 TR: Bogdan Chiuzbaian

Pg 83 BL: Kai Heeringa

Pg 83 BR: Heidi Adnum

Pg 85 L: Kyle Wong

Pg 85 TR & BR: Kristen Booth

Pg 87 L: La Redoute

Pg 87 TR : Kristen Booth

Pg 87 CR: Joshua Moïse

Pg 87 BR: Adam Weathered

Pg 88: Mark Molloy

Pg 89 T: Laksmi Dewi Siantar

Pg 89 B: Yifat Yogev Dadon

Pg 103 L: James Richardson

Pg 103 TR: Joshua Moïse

Pg 103 BR: Kristen Booth

Pg 105 L: Orlando Ricardo Ardana

Pg 105 TR: Anna Kim

Pg 105 BR: Kyle Wong

Pg 107 L: Kai Heeringa

Pg 107 TR: Kristen Booth

Pg 107 BR: Natascha Zivadinovic

Pg 109 L & TR: Lucy Smith

Pg 109 BR: La Redoute

Pg 110: La Redoute

Pg 111 T: Kai Heeringa

Pg 111 B: Cath Gersbeck

Pg 119 L: Heidi Adnum

Pg 119 TR: Paul Hance

Pg 119 BR: Kyle Wong

Pg 121 L: Ralene van der Walt

Pg 121 TR & BR: Cath Gersbeck

Pg 121 CR: Justyna Zdunczyk

Pg 123 L: Hobbs

Pg 123 TR: Jon Packard

Pg 123 BR: Kai Heeringa

Pg 124: EAST

Pg 125 T: Matt Harsevoort

Pg 125 B: Tiffany Ju

Pg 131 L: James Richardson

Pg 131 TR: Bodie Pierce

Pg 131 BR: Laksmi Dewi Siantar

Pg 133: La Redoute

Pg 135 L: Bogdan Chiuzbaian

Pg 135 TR: Matthew Miller

Pg 135 BR: Kai Heeringa

Pg 137 L: James Richardson

Pg 137 TR: Joe Kistel

Pg 137 BR: Julie Astrauckas

Pg 138: Kristen Booth

Pg 139 T: Kyle Wong

Pg 139 B: Rebecca Maynes

Pg 141: Paul Hance

Pg 145: Scott Roon

Pg 147: Sherry Heck

# INDEX

# ABOUT THE AUTHOR

Sewing expert and magazine editor Denise Wild is the Founder of LoveSewing and The Sewing Studio and the Content Director of BurdaStyle.

Denise started teaching sewing classes in her Toronto apartment in 2004 while she was working as an editor at Canada's top fashion publication. As her career in magazines grew, in turn so did her sewing classes. The classes evolved into The Sewing Studio New York, now North America's leading sewing school, and Denise merged her love of sewing with her passion for magazines by creating LoveSewing.com, the only sewing portal that focuses on fashion and style.

As well as overseeing LoveSewing and The Sewing Studio, Denise oversees the content of BurdaStyle North America including *BurdaStyle* magazine. "In the spring of 2013, I got an incredible call asking if I'd like to head up a new venture for the Burda brand across North America," says Denise. "Burda is known for being the leader in fashion sewing, and that's what drew me most to this role. Fashion has always been a very important part of my life, and I love to see the joy in other sewers (young and old, novice and veteran) when they create garments that are on-trend, that fit well, and that they can proudly boast, 'I made this!'

Before she became Editor of *BurdaStyle* magazine's US edition, Denise held senior editor and director titles at several top national publications including *FLARE*, *House & Home*, *Faze*, and *ANOKHI*, and has written for *Hello!*, *Elle*, *HGTV*, *W Network*, *Glow*, *Elevate*, *Chatelaine*, and *Slice*.

# ACKNOWLEDGMENTS

This book was written for anyone who's ever sat down at a sewing machine or held a needle and thread as well as those who are about to for the first time. I hope this book teaches you something new and inspires you to continue sewing and creating.

Sewing brings me incredible joy, and I hope that joy is carried to you through the words and pictures in this book!

First and foremost, I'd like to thank everyone who's ever taken a class at The Sewing Studio, everyone who's ever visited us on LoveSewing.com, and everyone who's been a part of our extended family over the years, including through social media. Thank you for sharing in my passion for sewing, thank you for your encouragement, and thank you for your excitement, enthusiasm, and your thirst for learning more.

A very special thank you to Nasya Newport, without whom this book would not have come together. Thank you for putting your heart and your soul into everything you do for me, for The Sewing Studio, and for LoveSewing. You really are an angel sent from heaven.

A huge thanks also to Rachel Simpson for doing such a great job at bringing this to life. Thank you for being an integral part of The Sewing Studio and LoveSewing every single day. I'm so appreciative of your dedication and your hard work.

Thank you to our entire TSS and LS family. I've had the extreme pleasure (and honor) of working with the most incredible team out there. The business and our students wouldn't be where they are today without you. My sincerest thanks to everyone involved day in and day out including our instructors, office staff, managers, editors, writers, designers, interns, freelancers, and collaborators, both past and present. You are the best!

Thank you to my mentor Doug Earle. Your wisdom, encouragement, faith, and support have guided me through many roads. Thank you for teaching me to only work with good people.

Thank you to all of my friends and family who have encouraged me throughout my journey in sewing and in business. And thank you to my very best friends, who never question me when I cancel dates because I'm working, but who instead cheer me on every step of the way.

Thank you to Isheeta Mustafi at RotoVision for sharing my vision and for getting *Mend & Make Fabulous* off the ground.

A heartfelt thank you to everyone involved behind-the-scenes of this book including Cath Senker and Allison Korleski who helped shape *Mend & Make Fabulous* to what it is, Madeleine Boardman, Heidi Adnum, Kin Hai, BD, RA, and Shane Mahood who filled these pages with the most beautiful images, and Portia Maunatlala, Nataly Garcia, Dominique Francis, Louise Sutton, and Julia Griaznova, who helped bring all of the pieces together in the very best way.

Finally, thank you to Interweave, BurdaStyle, and the entire F+W Media family for your faith in me and for your commitment to the love of sewing!

This book is dedicated to my mom (president of my fan club), my sister (my very best friend), and Roland (my one and only). The three of you inspire me every day to be loving, kind, and positive, to work hard, to have pride and integrity, and to settle for nothing but the best. I love you!